Woman Talk! The Encrypted Language Women Never Wanted Men To Know

Copyright © 2014 by Wilson Enterprises, LLC

No part of this publication may be reproduced, stored in a retrieval system, or transmitted in any form or by any means – electronic, mechanical, photocopy, recording, or any other – without the prior permission of the author.

ISBN: 978-0615884998

To my beautiful, smart, and understanding wife Lida. Without your support and guidance, I would not be half the man I am today.

Woman Talk!

The Encrypted Language Women Never Wanted Men To Know

Kevin S. Wilson P~~hD~~. **Married**

This book does not bash women (unless you like woman bashing books then go ahead and buy it), rather it is a comical look at the innate differences between men and women. Maybe that last sentence should be women and men to be PC. Anyway, my hopes are that both sexes will enjoy this book. At the end of your reading I hope you have a better understanding of the differences between the sexes. We as human beings can embrace these differences one of three ways. 1. Let little differences build up to such a point of frustration that they become big problems, 2. Let little differences build up to such a point of frustration that they result in assault and battery, 3. Acknowledge little differences as exactly what they are, little differences, and enjoy and accept these differences for they will always exist.

In reference to number one, this is probably a large reason for many relationship problems today. I am not a counselor or a psychologist so that's all I have to say about that. Number two probably violates some form of philosophical autonomy of being, besides, it just isn't very nice (not to mention any legal problems). Number three is what I believe to be the best objective outlook on this matter. If you agree, this book is for you. If you disagree, this book is definitely for you.

Woman Talk! Does it really exist? Is there a language that women have been keeping from men since the dawn of time? Can women communicate in a way that men do not understand? Are there certain thought patterns that are different in the male brain as opposed to the female brain? Let's try to find out as we explore "Woman Talk! The Encrypted Language Women Never Wanted Men To Know."

Table of Contents

Chapter 1:	In The Beginning…	8
Chapter 2:	Female Mathematics	16
Chapter 3:	Chapter 3	24
Chapter 4:	The Toilet Seat Test	36
Chapter 5:	Wait Before You Comment on Weight	50
Chapter 6:	If It Ain't Broke, Fix It	60
Chapter 7:	Driving	76
Chapter 8:	Educational Reading: Strategic Happiness	86
Chapter 9:	…In The End	108
Chapter 10:	Bonus Chapter: Strategic Happiness	114
	• Book Recommendations	115
	• Pie of Importance	119
	• Core Value Model	120
	• Life Mission Statement	121

Chapter 1
In The Beginning…

God created the world in six days and rested on the seventh. He (or She, sorry) then created life to inhabit the Earth. God created man in His/Her image, but something was still missing, so God took a rib from man (ouch!) and with it created woman. His name was Adam, and her name was Eve. Eve was to be the ideal companion for Adam, and they were to have lots and lots of children and live happily ever after.

This is the understanding of the beginning of "personkind," according to Christianity. A romantic and poetic explanation of how men and women were made for each other and how we are all brothers and sisters (actually now that I think about it, it sounds a little incestuous and disturbing). Nevertheless, this is our beginning.

Everything was going great! Adam was of the Earth, Eve was of Adam, and both of them were prancing around naked. Ah bliss! They had the run of the entire world, or at least a garden. They could do anything they wanted, except one thing. God told them not to eat the fruit of the tree of knowledge. One rule. Their only rule, and if they obeyed, life would continue to be great.

However, God messed up and added a tempting serpent to the story. This serpent, through his deviant and deceitful ways, talked Eve into taking an apple from the tree. Eve shared the apple with Adam, and together they made God very angry. God punished them for disobeying Him/Her in many ways, including having shame for their naked bodies. This, of course, meant leaves came into fashion, a part of the story still disappointing even to this day.

What does all of this mean, you say? My point is simple. That woman Eve messed everything up for everybody by taking the apple from that tree. (If you're a woman and you're still reading, good for you!) But MAN wrote the Bible. By blaming WOMAN for everything from the beginning, it is easy for man to maintain a sense of psychological and manipulative control over woman. By the way, my intentions here are not to create a controversy about religion or the book of God. My intention is simply to demonstrate a point about man and woman. If you are one of those who believe the Christian Bible is *actually written* by God and not man, please read my other book entitled "How God Did Not Write the Bible, Man Did."

All jokes aside, it is my belief that it was this beginning when the female gender created Woman Talk, and rightfully so. After blatantly being accused of causing all the hardships of humankind, I think it's only natural for women to plot a communicative alternative outside of man's ability. This wasn't too hard because, let's face it, man's abilities in the areas of effective communication are pretty slim. However, through time, patience, headaches, relationships, compiling, input, and a whole lot of other words, I have been fortunate enough to put together some of the pieces of this puzzle called Woman Talk.

Unfortunately, I don't have all the answers. Woman Talk is worse than computer software. Since its induction, there have been 3,521,124,546,568,546,612 versions. Some men start to figure out some of the language so women either have to kill them, or change the language. Since blood can stain clothes, they just thought it was easier to change it. This explains why so many versions exist. The networking procedure for this is either far advanced or way simple. So simple that you wouldn't even think of it, like turning to channel 11,921 on your television. I think it is more on a level of extra sensory projection with each other. Whatever it is, by the time it is changed, within three hours all women on the planet know it.

Since probably no man has all the answers, I am just going to provide a helpful guide on the basics of Woman Talk, the parts that are difficult to change. Use this information not as a manipulative tool but as a guide to better understand the female species. By the way, if I end up dead then you'll know I'm right on target, so avenge my death somehow.

To get an understanding of the induction of Woman Talk, we need an appreciation of the biological differences between men and women. It has been scientifically proven that we, as human beings, use a very small percentage of our brains. This is true for both men and women. I would never go so far as to say which gender uses more of their potential brain capacity. That would be suicide no matter which gender I chose. Rather, I would like to focus on the different areas of the brains the genders use. Different areas of the brain affect the way we think and perceive (or fail to think and perceive). Many of us already know this and have attempted to adapt accordingly. Let's explore the use of the brain by looking at diagram 1, the human brain.

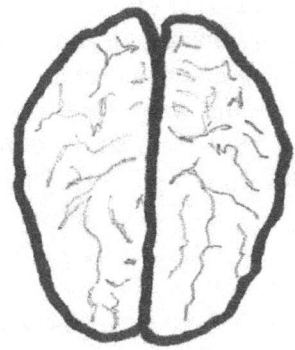

DIAGRAM 1, THE HUMAN BRAIN

As it is, the left side of the brain is better with facts, numbers, mechanics, reasoning, etc. The right side of the brain, however, is better with things like art, language, and music. This gives us a better understanding of how men and women interact. Let's first look at Man. In attempts to understand brain function and to oversimplify my point, I have made a diagram that shows on a percentage basis the amount of left side versus right side brain functions men use (See Diagram 2, The Brain of Man).

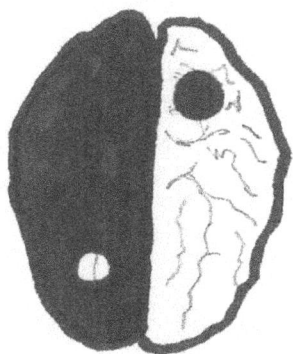

DIAGRAM 2, THE BRAIN OF MAN: 99% left, 1% right

It is clear to see which areas men spend most of their time in, and this wouldn't be a problem at all if men only had to relate to and communicate with other men. However, fortunately or unfortunately, men must also relate to and communicate with women. When we look at the brain of Woman, we start to get an understanding of why this process is sometimes so difficult (See Diagram 3, The Brain of Woman).

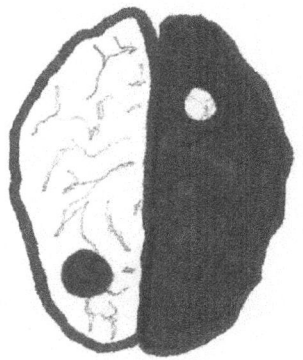

DIAGRAM 3, THE BRAIN OF WOMAN: 1% left, 99% right

Almost comical isn't it? Now, what does this mean for communication and relationships? I think we can best define this question with an example. Let's say a driver wants to get from point

A to destination point B. The driver is new to the area, so the driver stops to ask for directions. In scenario one, below, the driver asks a man for directions. In scenario two, the driver asks a woman for directions. Let's take a look at the outcomes.

Scenario One: Driver asks a man for directions

Driver: Excuse me?
Man: Yes?
Driver: I'm a little lost and I was wondering if you could help me?
Man: I will if I can, where are you headed?
Driver: Well, I need to get to Destination B.
Man: Oh, that's no problem. Do you know where Main Street is?
Driver: Yes, I do.
Man: Good, get back out on Main Street and head south. You will take Main Street for about 2 miles until you get to 62nd Street. Take a right on 62nd Street and continue heading west for about ½ mile to Franklin Street. Take a left on Franklin Street and continue south for 2 blocks. Destination B is the second building on the right on the 3rd block.

Scenario Two: Driver asks a woman for directions

Driver: Excuse me?
Woman: Yes?
Driver: I'm a little lost and I was wondering if you could help me?
Woman: I will if I can, where are you headed?
Driver: Well, I need to get to Destination B.
Woman: Oh, that's no problem. Do you know where Main Street is?
Driver: Yes, I do.
Woman: Good, get back out on Main Street and head in the direction of the large water tower. Drive towards the water tower for about one and a half songs on the radio until you get to the Dairy Queen. It's the Dairy Queen with the red roof, not the one with the blue roof that is on the other side of town. Anyway, go right at the street right in front of the Dairy Queen. You will drive on that street for about half of a song. You will pass by a house with a tall iron fence out front. When you see that house you are half way there. Keep going

until you see the red brick house with a tall chimney on the back side of the house. Turn left on the first street you come to after you pass that red brick house. Drive on that street and you will see a big yard with a white picket fence and a large black dog in the yard. The dog is sometimes in the back not in the front. You still need to go until you see that yard though, the one with the white picket fence. After you get to that fence you're almost there. Keep going and you'll see Destination B next to the big tall oak tree. It is the one with a flat roof, not the one with the pointed roof.

Now, whether or not the driver reaches Destination B depends on one thing – whether the driver is a man or a woman. If the driver is a woman and gets Scenario One directions, she will most likely seek out the directions from another woman. If the driver is a man and gets Scenario Two directions, he will most likely roll up the car window, scream, suddenly develop a headache, and drive around aimlessly at alarming speeds until he works out where Destination B is on his own. This second example is, of course, absurd because you and I both know that men never ask for directions. This type of uncontrollable behavior could be part of the reason why. Another part of the reason why is also gender based, but in a different way.

Whenever a man asks another man for directions, the man he asks is extremely put out and answers in a less than sincere way. He doesn't dare ask a woman for directions in fear of an answer like Scenario Two. If a woman (especially an attractive one) asks a man for directions, chances are the man will stop what he's doing, get in his car, and have her follow him to the destination. He doesn't know why he does this, he just does. If a woman asks another woman for directions, the other woman is sympathetic and gives directions that are sincere and offered in a manner mutually understandable (it is a rule in the Woman Talk Code that they have to do this).

All of these different scenarios simply have to do with left brain versus right brain usage, and I'm glad we have these differences. If we lived in an "equal usage" world, it would be a utopian world of clear communication and total understanding, and who would want that?

If you have trouble believing these differences then I have a test for you. If you have a partner, try lying to them. Now understand, I don't normally condone lying, but for this test I think it is okay. The results of this test should come out the same every time. If you are a man lying to a woman, she knows that you are lying. If you are a woman lying to a man, he doesn't have a clue. She could tell him that the tower of Pisa is leaning because the stairs were built only on one side, and he'd believe it. The reason for this is a simple one. Because of the right- and left-brain usage, men and women hold uniquely different perspectives on their environment. Women are aware of their environment more holistically than men are. Therefore, when a man lies, women are able to hear the lie in his voice, see it in his eyes, read it in his movement, see it on his lips, feel it in their hearts, and read it on his forehead. With this holistic approach, men don't stand a chance.

When a woman lies to a man, all the man is able to interpret are the words that he hears, "No, I did not spend $ 1,000 on shoes last week. You must have done it and then forgot about it." Now, since a man is only able to interpret the words that he hears, and those words said "no," more than likely he will assume he spent the money on shoes and then forgot about it (since his memory is not so good anyway). His memory can't be good since he doesn't even remember where he put all those shoes.

This scenario, of course, may be a little disturbing to read if you're a man. If you're a woman, then you know this and have undoubtedly taken advantage of it from time to time (only in your *past* relationships, of course). Fellow men, there is one point in this situation that should bring you comfort; there is nothing you can do to improve on this. We will always be literal and linear thinkers, which helped us get by until now so why change it. Because of our linear thinking, man has always had a desire to formulate and organize. We've added regularity and structure into a once unknown universe. From Socrates to Aristotle, Galileo to Newton, we have been able to unlock mysteries for future generations to build upon. Our greatest asset in the unraveling of these mysteries is through the use of what we call mathematics. This system comforts us, or so we thought.

I've got news for you guys. You're unaware of another system out there. Actually, you may be partially aware of it and just not know how it works. It is not mathematics, but rather Female Mathematics, and it is more involved than you can possibly imagine.

Chapter 2
Female Mathematics

    Mathematics! The universal language that leaves no room for controversy, question, or interpretation. Two plus two is indeed equal to four. This is fact. I do, however, remember one of my college professors mentioning a 400-page book that explains how this simple equation is proven. At this point in my life though, I'm willing just to accept it as truth. If I have two apples and add two more apples, then I have four apples. Or was that, if I have two apples and then add two oranges, I have four pieces of fruit? Oh, the hell with it; two plus two IS equal to four.
    Over the years, we as a species developed our understanding of mathematics in order to accomplish amazing things. Architecture, computers, space exploration – mathematics was there. From its angles and measurements to its one's and zero's, mathematics is certainly woven into our fabric of life. It is hard to imagine a time without it. How its uses evolved. How its processes are learned. Addition, subtraction, division, multiplication, algebra, geometry, trigonometry, calculus. Could you imagine having to learn it all over again?
    Well, I've got bad news for you. You do.
    There is a mathematical system out there that I like to call "Female Mathematics" (not really a very original name I'm afraid). I didn't actually become aware of its existence until after I was married. It is, for the most part, pretty cleverly covered up.
    It was probably less than a year into my marriage when I began to see it. Everything was going great, as it still is (thank God) today. I was 26 or 27 at the time and leased a building that I taught Martial Arts classes out of. My wife worked out in my facility in a Cardio Kickboxing class that we had, so she was up there pretty regularly. She really seemed to enjoy the class, kicking, punching,

sparring..... as I reflect, I probably never should have told her about that class. Anyway, that's beside the point.

At this dojo (martial arts school), we had a lot of kid's classes. Now let me tell you, if you ever want a lesson in patience, try teaching kids. If I had grade school to do all over again (I'd kill myself), I would have let those teachers know what a great job they were doing. It's honestly amazing that many kids walk away learning anything, by no fault of the teacher. There can be so many distractions, yelling, running, squirming, spitting, slapping, teasing, pushing; sorry, I kind of got on an "ing" thing there for a minute. What I'm saying is it can be a real challenge. I was fortunate that in my karate classes, most of the kids wanted to be there, and they only had to have solid attention for about an hour (not to mention we could kick or punch them if they got out of line and it was considered part of the curriculum).

One day, an order came in from one of my students. She was in Girl Scouts, and some time back asked me if I wanted to buy cookies. She was quite the salesperson; it was really hard to get me to buy food (right, I'd eat the box they came in if I got hungry enough). Her tactic was, "Do you want to buy some cookies?" I said, "Yes!" Anyway, the cookies came in finally, and she brought them up to the school. Being the nice guy I am, I shared them with some of the other instructors. My wife caught a break during the class and came over to try one of the cookies. Yes, since we'd been married she was testing her boundaries in the rights of the unity of two people.

After her first bite, she was in heaven. It was a delicious cookie indeed, and she was quick to say, "Save me one." Now, let's take a look at this statement, and remember I am a man. I am a simple, linear, literal thinker. Be particular about the things you say to me, for I can only do what I actually hear. "Save me ONE!"

Oh that cookie was so hard to save. At first I just left it out on the counter for her, but I am a weak man. If I didn't move this cookie, I would fail at her wish, to save her one. So I moved the cookie into the cabinet, but that was no good for I still knew it was there. I tried to hide the cookie from myself. After all, being a man, my memory wasn't so good. So what I did was put the cookie in a place that I would never expect it to be, and then tried to forget about it. Funny thing about memory, if you try to forget something, you

NEVER will. Besides that, it didn't take me to long to figure out that if I had been successful in this, there would be a mean search and recovery operation right in our own household.

I put the cookie back in the cabinet. I tried to think of things like fruits and vegetables, but that just made me want the cookie even more. After a little household work, I began to take my mind off of the cookie. (When I say household work I do mean household work. Sweeping, mopping, wiping, vacuuming – I am unlike most men in this regard, and, no, I am not gay-not that there is anything wrong with that.)

Finally, the time came to present the cookie to my wife, Lida. Moment of triumph, or so I thought. At this moment I quickly became aware of two things. Number one, it's not wise to upset a woman, and number two – Female Mathematics. Depending upon your gender, you are probably looking at this scenario one of two ways. Scenario number one, man perspective: "Save me one cookie." Through great sacrifice, struggle, torment, and strong will, I saved that cookie. I wanted to eat that cookie so badly. Sure the other thirty-nine or so were good, but I had a sneaking suspicion that this number forty cookie was going to taste even better. However, I didn't eat it. I saved it because my wife asked me to, and she was counting on me doing so. Yea for me, yea for MAN!

Scenario number two, woman perspective: "You asshole, you only saved me ONE cookie!"

I don't think I need to tell you what an utter disappointment this was to both genders. I mean here I was, on the top of self-discipline mountain, only to find out the markings were wrong and it was actually the mountain of self-centeredness (surely a man put up the markings in the first place, and then was killed by a woman before he got a chance to take them down after realizing his mistake). And here she was, with only one cookie.

Now here's when the mathematics of "femality" comes in. I don't even pretend to have all of the answers, but I have been able to start a foundation based off of this particular circumstance. The foundation is this, $1 \geq 2$. That's right, you heard it here first, these are the building blocks of what I have come to call "Female Mathematics" (patent pending). After I started breathing again (air pressure changes after rapidly coming down one mountain then immediately up another one), I tried to explain to my wife the simplicity of the situation. "Honey," I said "you tried a cookie, said it was good, then asked me to save you ONE, ONE cookie you said. I did precisely what you asked. I mean you asked for ONE cookie, I saved you ONE cookie. I have done nothing wrong here. I mean, you look mad, but you're not mad, you CAN'T be mad, I did EXACTLY what you asked. I saved you ONE! There it is, I did my job. I didn't say ONE, you did, I did what YOU said."

Now believe it or not, she accused me of being sarcastic at this point. Reflecting on it now, I can see why she might have thought that. I'm here to tell you, though, that was truly not my intention or the tone I wanted to set (believe that). I was simply equating a simple formula I learned early on in my education, and that is $1 = 1$. Upon further investigation, I did find out this simply isn't true all the time. This was because she told me when she said one, she meant at least two. I started to say that if you wanted two you should have said two, but I figured that sarcasm thing would come up again. I controlled myself and kept my mouth shut.

As I said, this is only the foundation, and as the mathematical equation advances, it would really look more like this: $1 \geq 2$ some of the time. I further broke this down, and in its truest form, it looks something like this: $1 \geq 2$ when it works to my advantage. This is the trouble with Female Mathematics – it is set up so men cannot compute favorable outcomes. It's kind of like putting a dollar into a change machine and getting back three quarters. In trying to exchange those three quarters back for your dollar, you get five dimes. You cannot win.

As you can imagine, this complex system is difficult to track. Maybe impossible. To truly understand this math you will have to commit more than just your free time (or just be a woman). I'll provide some examples to get you started, and if you get frustrated and develop a small headache (or large one), you're probably on the right track.

Cookie counting is pretty obvious. Even a man can understand the concept of getting more than you ask for. The underlying question that has to be addressed here is why not ask for the amount that you want? And why will a woman ask for one cookie, but not ask for two? This is because if she asks for one cookie, she is simply a curious part of the population who would like to explore the savory taste of one harmless cookie. If she asks for two, she is big, fat, greedy pig. Now I know this concept is absurd, but it's the way women think (and don't try denying it if you're a woman). It is up to the man in this situation (or any situation that has to deal with food) to know and to sensitively understand that $1 \geq 2$.

This equation can also be true with money. However, with money we have to incorporate special circumstances. For example, if a woman asks you for one dollar, you better give her at least two. If she asks for two dollars, you better give her at least four, and you'd probably be better of just giving her a five (don't compute that, just trust me on this one).

When it comes to the giving and receiving of money, there is a doubling and halving rule that simply must apply. If a man gives a woman money per her request, he should take the amount she asked for and double it. This is standard; it's no big accomplishment on the side of the man. It is simply what's expected. If a man asks a woman for money (by the way, I don't recommend this), expect half of what you ask for. And don't you dare ask for double what you really want, because somehow she'll know. I am convinced, by the way, that some department stores have this double/half button on their registers. They usually try to pacify the state of shock with some explanation about tax, and it usually works because the shock rarely wears off before you leave the store. Be careful where you shop and the company you shop with.

These have, for the most part, been mathematical equations that increase in numbers. She asks for one and gets two. Asks for two and gets four, and so on. We now must look at the diminishing side of numbers. Rounding is a very useful tool in math. It can be used to simplify computations. Numbers that show up between two integers become an integer by simply going to the closest one, up or down. Very convenient at times it is. You drove 78.4 miles, so we'll just call it 78, or even perhaps 80. Sure there's some relativity involved in rounding, but it's an estimate, an approximation. No one cares that you ran a mile in 4 minutes and 33.43784655384658 seconds; you ran it in 4 minutes and 33 seconds, period (and damn you for running so fast anyway; did you have a dog chasing you or something?). It is much simpler this way for many things. Women use this rounding tool quite a bit. The only problem is, the tool of relativity decides whether or not the rounding is to their advantage, or to their disadvantage.

Let's go back to the money example. Say a blouse on the rack is $ 24.99. It's a beautiful blouse, one of a kind, just what your wife (or significant other) has been searching for and hasn't found since she started looking ten years ago. So, of course, she has to buy it. God Him/Herself put that blouse there for her to see. To deny purchasing that blouse would be the same as denying God. Okay, I can live with that. Men are sometimes impulsive buyers too. The problem comes when you ask her how much she spent. This is where rounding comes into play. I wouldn't expect an answer of $24.99, I mean, you can round. The question is which way to round. Does she go ahead and round up with that one little penny to $25.00, or does she round down to $ 24.00? The answer should be obvious. NEITHER! This blouse, with a purchase price of $24.99, somehow gets rounded down to $ 20.00. Now how the hell does that work? The real kicker is you gave her $49.98 to buy it (and if you really gave her $ 49.98 to buy it and not $ 50.00, then you're not really paying attention).

Let's look at another rounding situation (again relative to advantage and disadvantage). Did you know that it is impossible to gain a pound if you're a woman? That's right, impossible. You can only gain fractions of pounds. She didn't gain a pound, she gained a half a pound, or a quarter of a pound, or 0.00018745635^{th} of a pound (yes, scales are pretty accurate these days, I never knew that little dial could be so precise). On the opposite end, if a woman loses 0.0000000000000000000000001 of a pound, we'll just call that losing one pound. We will deal more with weight in Chapter 5: *Wait Before You Comment On Weight*. It is a very important chapter, and one should not attempt to compute weight (or at least say anything out loud) until reading this chapter. I mean it. I'm not joking. If you're not careful, you'll be counting stars rather than pounds (you can use traditional mathematics for stars).

I think this is the reason actual mathematics was created in the first place. It takes out the relativity factor. Men are always messing up, and rarely truly sensitive to the needs or wants of a woman. Math gives them an undeniably correct outcome. The information goes in, and an answer comes out. This is the way that we like it, simple, linear, literal. I mean, we like to be right sometimes too. I'm sure it's difficult to imagine if you're a woman what it must be like to be wrong all the time. It's very taxing. It is not difficult to figure out why men put forth little effort when it comes to helping out with women's needs. I'm sure it is where the phrase "damned if you do, damned if you don't" came from.

Take, for example, my wife and me. We do have a special relationship. We have the ability to recognize each other's strengths and weaknesses. Where I am weak, she tries to be strong. Where she is strong, I try to be weak. Wait a minute. I think that's how she tells it. You know what I mean. Seriously, there is a strong synergy between us most of the time. Problems arise when I try to cross over and do something I shouldn't be messing with, some area I am weak in, say laundry. Before I was married, I had a specific way of doing laundry – wash everything in cold. This system never failed me. There was no sorting by color, by size, by fabric, there was only dirty or clean. The dirty clothes went in the washer with cold water, and the clean clothes went in the pile of clean clothes. After a few years I even got advanced and starting putting laundry detergent in with the clothes and cold water. After I got married, I discovered there was an alternative method for washing clothes out there, one that my wife preferred to mine.

I would love to tell you what this alternative method for washing clothes is, but I simply don't know. It seems as if when I think I have it figured out, it changes (I'm starting to think this is purposeful). The simplest solution I've found for this is to let her do the laundry, all the time, every time. See where this is going. The thing is, this is an area that she is stronger in than I am. This unfortunately does not grant me immunity from ever doing the laundry. I remember one time recently when Lida was working a lot, and the laundry was piling up. Like a dummy I told her that I would take care of it. I made sure I went through a list of particulars such as water temperature, detergent amount, fabric softener amount, separation, what dries in the dryer, what dries on its own, what time to do it, what stage the moon should be in, you know, the usual. I had what I thought was complete clarification. The only thing she mentioned on top of what I said was not to wash any sweaters. This seemed simple enough, until I went to do the laundry.

It was then that I realized that I was in a no-win situation. I came upon a piece of clothing, let's call it a sweater. Now, I say let's call it a sweater because I didn't know if it was a sweater or not. It seemed to be made of a sweater-like material, only it had short sleeves. I don't know of many sweaters that have short sleeves, but I became very curious at this point. What really threw me was this: if this wasn't a sweater, then there were no sweaters at all in the pile of laundry, and she said not to wash any sweaters. If you are reading this and you are thinking through it logically, then right now you are saying to yourself "just don't wash the piece of clothing you think is a sweater." This is what I was thinking at first, too, but you see, I'm smarter than that. I was in a no-win situation. I was "damned if I do, damned if I don't."

For those of you having a hard time following, let me break it down for you. If I wash this "sweater" and it turns out that it is a sweater, I think you can understand the problem with that. After all, the only specific instruction she gave me was not to wash any sweaters. So the safe thing to do is not wash it, but this has problems of its own. If it turns out this article is NOT a sweater, then it will turn out to be the one piece of clothing she was planning to wear the day after laundry was done. Since it wasn't washed, it must now wait to be washed with the next cycle of dirty clothing because all the other clothes are now clean. Should I attempt to explain that I thought it was a sweater, and I didn't want to ruin it based off her explanation, she kindly calls me an idiot and explains that, for future reference, sweaters have sleeves. If you took a chance and washed it, she'll ask you why the hell you washed a sweater after she specifically told you not to wash any sweaters.

So you see, there is no way to win. Seemingly, the only way to win is to avoid offering to do the laundry at all, but this is a farce because not offering is losing too. I think it's because of situations like these that man created mathematics to begin with. As I said, it's nice to be right sometimes. I remember I was right about something back in 1982, and, oh boy, it felt good. Someday maybe I'll feel that way again.

Chapter 3
Chapter 3

I don't know what the hell the meaning of this chapter title is. I truly think I would have to be a woman to get this. I am basically talking about communicative language here. In its basic form, Chapter 3 simply means the 3rd chapter in your reading of this book. However, if you repeat it, then it means something entirely different. I haven't figured out what, but whatever it is, it's exponential in nature. For example, Chapter 3, Chapter 3 would be something like Chapter 16. I don't know why you wouldn't just say Chapter 16, but I'm a man so I'm not meant to understand.

Probably the most common use of this repetitive, exponential, translation, speaking can be found in teenage girls. You see, they can like a boy, but it's entirely different if they *like, like* the boy. That means something like they love him, or at least like him a whole lot. This is most of the time used in the opposite form. "Julie, what do you think of Tommy?" "Well, I like him, but I don't like, like him." Does this sound at all familiar?

This concept can be used with many words. For example, if something is scalding hot, then it is hot, hot. If something is gigantically tall, then it is tall, tall. If someone is really dumb, then he's dumb, dumb (this over the years has been changed to "a" dumb, dumb). This concept is not entirely difficult to figure out; it is more the wondering why it is done that confuses most men.

Language in general is a beautiful thing. It is wonderful to be able to communicate one's thoughts, emotions, feelings, or desires to another human being in a way that there is a camaraderie of understanding and sharing. If you don't realize this, try being surrounded by people speaking a foreign language for a while.

My wife is from the Czech Republic. She moved here when she was about 25. She did not speak much English at all when she first arrived in the U.S. (fortunately she spoke plenty when we met). After we were married, we went one Christmas to visit her family in

Prague. It was the first time I was meeting them, and I was a little anxious (especially once I stepped off the plane). My wife did great, though, at keeping me in the conversations, especially since none of her family spoke any English.

The inevitable eventually did occur. A couple of days after we had been there, her father and stepmother were giving us a ride to her mother's apartment. My wife and her stepmother decided they wanted to stop at the drug store. Under normal circumstances, this wouldn't be a big deal. However, these were not normal circumstances.

There were two of us left in the car at this point, her father and myself. He spoke Czech, and I spoke English – not much to talk about. Now I'll be honest with you, we were probably only in that car together for a total of four minutes. Time, like many things, is extremely relative. If I'm ever on my deathbed and have only four minutes left to live, just put me in a car with a man who doesn't speak my language. I will then live the equivalent of two more lifetimes before I perish. That was how long it seemed to be when I sat there in the car with her father. It really sucked, sucked.

Now sure, I could have spoken to him. I could have said hello, good-bye, salt please, and, of course, I could have cussed at him. It didn't seem that any of these would be appropriate at the time. So there I sat, each second passing by like an hour, praying for something to break the silence. Finally, he turns back and looks at me. He points across the street. At first I didn't know what he was pointing at. I didn't realize until he said the words "my first car." He was pointing to a Volks Wagen Bug. I'll tell you, I never thought three little words could sound so good. We must have sat there and repeated the word Bug at least twenty times, but I didn't care, it was at least something to break the silence.

You can see how advantageous communication and language is. For this reason, I suppose, for the most part, we should be thankful. Usually, men and women have a generally similar communicative process. I suppose repeating a word and changing its meaning isn't so bad. If that were the only communicative barrier.

Unfortunately for us men, this is not the only barrier we face. As I mentioned before, women are much more holistic in thinking, and complex by nature. This is hard for us because this means women can talk about one thing but mean something else. This makes it quite difficult to understand what the hell women are talking about, which is exactly the way they want it.

This enables them to communicate with each other right in front of you without you having any idea what is being said. I don't think I need to explain to you how advantageous this system is for them. Probably the hardest part about this whole situation is to be cool. The coolest, smartest, fastest-witted guy in the world can be turned into a bumbling idiot when trying to follow a female conversation. This doesn't exactly stroke the male ego. And it, of course, doesn't even take into effect alternative means of communication, like body posture, eye queues, or mental telepathy. Once these are implemented, all understanding for man is simply lost.

After piecing much of this together, I decided to share an example of how this works. If you're a man trying to follow this, you may have to reread it a few times before you get it. If you're a woman trying to follow this, I know you'll get it, and try to deny its validity. I'm truly sorry for exposing this example, but am fairly confident your communicative process will remain safe.

A man and a woman are having a conversation. The topic of this conversation has to do with another woman. The woman in this conversation is trying to set this man up with this other woman. It is no big secret what a man looks for in a woman when they first go out; don't forget we're simple creatures. Women know this, so if they are trying to set a woman up who is less than desirable, the talk would go something like this:

> Woman: You should meet my friend Susie. You'd really like her.
>
> Man: Well, what is she like?
>
> Woman: Oh, you'd like her. She's a lot of fun. She has a great personality, you guys like the same things, and she's really nice.

I suppose at this point we should get into translation. With enough persistence from the woman, the man would probably go out with the other woman. If he paid closer attention, though, he probably could have avoided what is inevitably going to be a catastrophe. Let's look at the first statement.

> Woman: You should meet my friend Susie. You'd really like her.

Red flag. The intent of the woman in this situation is not to make the man happy, but rather to make her friend happy. What this statement is really saying is, "My friend Susie would really like you." Her true interest is not the man. Men are so self-centered we fall for this right away and believe the woman's intentions are directed toward us. Let's now look at the man's response.

> Man: Well, what is she like?

No big secret here. A grasshopper could figure out what this statement is really saying, and that is "What does she look like?" Let's look at the woman's response.

> Woman: Oh, you'd like her. She's a lot of fun. She has a great personality, you guys like the same things, and she's really nice.

Okay, let's look at the first part. "Oh, you'd like her," this, of course, goes back to the scenario of she would like him. Next part, "She is a lot of fun" can't be at all true. The mere fact that she would point this out right away means it cannot be true. What this really means is that she is reserved and doesn't get out much. If she did, she would probably be there right now. "She has a great personality" is an easy one. This simply means she is ugly. "You guys like the same things" is another easy one; the man will learn to like the same things she does. "And she's really nice" means she's a real bitch that no man can stand to be with more than twenty minutes.

So why is it that women aren't just more forthcoming when it comes to setting up their friends? Quite simply, no man would go out with a woman if her friend described her as she really was. Just listen to the sentence. "Oh, she'd like you. She's not much fun and doesn't get out much. Most men would consider her ugly, you'd have to learn to like the things she likes, and she's a real bitch toward men." Oh, please, can I be the first to go out with her?

This indirectness is common with women. If they're indirect and it is okay with another woman, this is called friendship. If they're indirect and it is not okay with another woman, it is then called two-faced. It's rather difficult to keep it all straight.

In terms of two-faced, I have finally figured out why it is women travel in groups to the bathroom. Surely you've witnessed this. I always thought they helped each other somehow. What did I know? I've discovered a distinct reason they travel in groups. The real reason is they don't want things said about them if one goes alone. Whether in a group of men, women, or both, a woman knows her "friends" can become "two-faced" with very little influence. To keep things safe, they just all go to the bathroom together. Now you know.

You may notice some of these things in everyday life. If you're a man and you don't notice, then you were not meant to. Everything that is done is done for a reason. The male gender is not supposed to know the reason. Even if we did know the reason, we wouldn't understand it. That is how lost we are. We simply do not get it, and that's just the way the women like it. There are certain measures put in place to control us. They control what we think, what we say, how we act, and so on. Don't believe me? Try this little test.

If you have a significant other, imagine you're out shopping together. I realize this is a rare occurrence, but just humor me a little bit. Let's say you're a man. You're out shopping for an article of clothing with your significant other (and, of course. I mean an article of clothing for her). All of a sudden, you see one of your long-lost friends. You haven't seen them for a long time, so you want to take the opportunity to talk a little, catch up if you will (besides, it beats the hell out of shopping). You do this; you are confident, talkative, nostalgic. Why shouldn't you be? This is a good friend you haven't seen in a long time. What could possibly keep you from being all these things? I'll tell you what, one simple little five-letter word, p-u-r-s-e purse.

Take the same situation, only now you're standing outside the changing room holding "the purse." I don't care who you are, how secure you think you might be in your manhood, it changes the way you feel when you hold "the purse." You go from being confident, secure, and talkative to passive, shy, and avoidant. No matter how cool you think you are, you just cannot keep your cool status when you're holding "the purse." Do you think it is by accident they take the smallest, cutest, daintiest one when you go shopping together? Of course not. They know that at some point you will be holding it, and they want you to have "the feeling." "The feeling" goes hand in hand with "the purse." What it is designed to do, is put you in your place. Just when you feel as if you're on top of the world, that nothing or no one could bring you down. When you feel as if you could take on anything or anyone. When there is no situation that would dare think of not being conquered by you. They quickly remind you they can destroy that confidence and those feelings ... with a little purse.

It's all part of the game, the dance, the control. Language takes on new meanings when we tweak it just a little bit. Doubling up words takes on whole new meanings. Code words convey real meanings. Psychological measures are used to take control of our thoughts, our ideas, and even our understanding of our very existence. All of it is done just to keep us in their grips (and, of course, to give them something to laugh at). Based upon these revelations, I have just one thing to say to you concerning this chapter.

If you thought this chapter was good, then was it really good or good, good? Whatever the hell that means. If you thought this chapter was bad, then we'll just call it good.

Chapter 3
Chapter 3

(This chapter repeats itself in exactly the same form. I don't know what it will mean, mean if you read it a second time. If you don't want to find out, go ahead and move on to chapter 4). I don't know what the hell the meaning of this chapter title is. I truly think I would have to be a woman to get this. I am basically talking about communicative language here. In its basic form, Chapter 3 simply means the 3rd chapter in your reading of this book. However, if you repeat it, then it means something entirely different. I haven't figured out what, but whatever it is, it's exponential in nature. For example, Chapter 3, Chapter 3 would be something like Chapter 16. I don't know why you wouldn't just say Chapter 16, but I'm a man so I'm not meant to understand.

Probably the most common use of this repetitive, exponential, translation, speaking can be found in teenage girls. You see, they can like a boy, but it's entirely different if they *like, like* the boy. That means something like they love him, or at least like him a whole lot. This is most of the time used in the opposite form. "Julie, what do you think of Tommy?" "Well, I like him, but I don't like, like him." Does this sound at all familiar?

This concept can be used with many words. For example, if something is scalding hot, then it is hot, hot. If something is gigantically tall, then it is tall, tall. If someone is really dumb, then he's dumb, dumb (this over the years has been changed to "a" dumb, dumb). This concept is not entirely difficult to figure out; it is more the wondering why it is done that confuses most men.

Language in general is a beautiful thing. It is wonderful to be able to communicate one's thoughts, emotions, feelings, or desires to another human being in a way that there is a camaraderie of understanding and sharing. If you don't realize this, try being surrounded by people speaking a foreign language for a while.

My wife is from the Czech Republic. She moved here when she was about 25. She did not speak much English at all when she first arrived in the U.S. (fortunately she spoke plenty when we met). After we were married, we went one Christmas to visit here family in Prague. It was the first time I was meeting them, and I was a little anxious (especially once I stepped off the plane). My wife did great, though, at keeping me in the conversations, especially since none of her family spoke any English.

The inevitable eventually did occur. A couple of days after we had been there, her father and stepmother were giving us a ride to her mother's apartment. My wife and her stepmother decided they wanted to stop at the drug store. Under normal circumstances, this wouldn't be a big deal. However, these were not normal circumstances.

There were two of us left in the car at this point, her father and myself. He spoke Czech, and I spoke English – not much to talk about. Now I'll be honest with you, we were probably only in that car together for a total of four minutes. Time, like many things, is extremely relative. If I'm ever on my deathbed and have only four minutes left to live, just put me in a car with a man who doesn't speak my language. I will then live the equivalent of two more lifetimes before I perish. That was how long it seemed to be when I sat there in the car with her father. It really sucked, sucked.

Now sure, I could have spoken to him. I could have said hello, good-bye, salt please, and, of course, I could have cussed at him. It didn't seem that any of these would be appropriate at the time. So there I sat, each second passing by like an hour, praying for something to break the silence. Finally, he turns back and looks at me. He points across the street. At first I didn't know what he was pointing at. I didn't realize until he said the words "my first car." He was pointing to a Volks Wagen Bug. I'll tell you, I never thought three little words could sound so good. We must have sat there and repeated the word Bug at least twenty times, but I didn't care, it was at least something to break the silence.

You can see how advantageous communication and language is. For this reason, I suppose, for the most part, we should be thankful. Usually, men and women have a generally similar communicative process. I suppose repeating a word and changing its meaning isn't so bad. If that were the only communicative barrier.

Unfortunately for us men, this is (are you *really* still reading this?) not the only barrier we face. As I mentioned before, women are much more holistic in thinking, and complex by nature. This is hard for us because this means women can talk about one thing but mean something else. This makes it quite difficult to understand what the hell women are talking about, which is exactly the way they want it.

This enables them to communicate with each other right in front of you without you having any idea what is being said. I don't think I need to explain to you how advantageous this system is for them. Probably the hardest part about this whole situation is to be cool. The coolest, smartest, fastest-witted guy in the world can be turned into a bumbling idiot when trying to follow a female conversation. This doesn't exactly stroke the male ego. And it, of course, doesn't even take into effect alternative means of communication, like body posture, eye queues, or mental telepathy. Once these are implemented, all understanding for man is simply lost.

After piecing much of this together, I decided to share an example of how this works. If you're a man trying to follow this, you may have to reread it a few times before you get it. If you're a woman trying to follow this, I know you'll get it, and try to deny its validity. I'm truly sorry for exposing this example, but am fairly confident your communicative process will remain safe.

A man and a woman are having a conversation. The topic of this conversation has to do with another woman. The woman in this conversation is trying to set this man up with this other woman. It is no big secret what a man looks for in a woman when they first go out; don't forget we're simple creatures. Women know this, so if they are trying to set a woman up who is less than desirable, the talk would go something like this:

Woman: You should meet my friend Susie. You'd really like her.

Man: Well, what is she like?

> Woman: Oh, you'd like her. She's a lot of fun. She has a great personality, you guys like the same things, and she's really nice.

I suppose at this point we should get into translation. With enough persistence from the woman, the man would probably go out with the other woman. If he paid closer attention, though, he probably could have avoided what is inevitably going to be a catastrophe. Let's look at the first statement.

> Woman: You should meet my friend Susie. You'd really like her.

Red flag. The intent of the woman in this situation is not to make the man happy, but rather to make her friend happy. What this statement is really saying is, "My friend Susie would really like you." Her true interest is not the man. Men are so self-centered we fall for this right away and believe the woman's intentions are directed toward us. Let's now look at the man's response.

> Man: Well, what is she like?

No big secret here. A grasshopper could figure out what this statement is really saying, and that is "What does she look like?" Let's look at the woman's response.

> Woman: Oh, you'd like her. She's a lot of fun. She has a great personality, you guys like the same things, and she's really nice.

Okay, let's look at the first part. "Oh, you'd like her," this, of course, goes back to the scenario of she would like him. Next part, "She is a lot of fun" can't be at all true. The mere fact that she would point this out right away means it cannot be true. What this really means is that she is reserved and doesn't get out much. If she did, she would probably be there right now. "She has a great personality" is an easy one. This simply means she is ugly. "You guys like the same things" is another easy one; the man will learn to like the same things she does. "And she's really nice" means she's a real bitch that no man can stand to be with more than twenty minutes.

So why is it that women aren't just more forthcoming when it comes to setting up their friends? Quite simply, no man would go out with a woman if her friend described her as she really was. Just listen to the sentence. "Oh, she'd like you. She's not much fun and doesn't get out much. Most men would consider her ugly, you'd have to learn to like the things she likes, and she's a real bitch toward men." Oh, please, can I be the first to go out with her?

This indirectness is common with women. If they're indirect and it is okay with another woman, this is called friendship. If they're indirect and it is not okay with another woman, it is then called two-faced. It's rather difficult to keep it all straight.

In terms of two-faced, I have finally figured out why it is women travel in groups to the bathroom. Surely you've witnessed this. I always thought they helped each other somehow. What did I know? I've discovered a distinct reason they travel in groups. The real reason is they don't want things said about them if one goes alone. Whether in a group of men, women, or both, a woman knows her "friends" can become "two-faced" with very little influence. To keep things safe, they just all go to the bathroom together. Now you know.

You may notice some of these things in everyday life. If you're a man and you don't notice, then you were not meant to. Everything that is done is done for a reason. The male gender is not supposed to know the reason. Even if we did know the reason, we wouldn't understand it. That is how lost we are. We simply do not get it, and that's just the way the women like it. There are certain measures put in place to control us. They control what we think, what we say, how we act, and so on. Don't believe me? Try this little test.

If you have a significant other, imagine you're out shopping together. I realize this is a rare occurrence, but just humor me a little bit. Let's say you're a man. You're out shopping for an article of clothing with your significant other (and, of course. I mean an article of clothing for her). All of a sudden, you see one of your long-lost friends. You haven't seen them for a long time, so you want to take the opportunity to talk a little, catch up if you will (besides, it beats the hell out of shopping). You do this; you are confident, talkative, nostalgic. Why shouldn't you be? This is a good friend you haven't seen in a long time. What could possibly keep you from being all these things? I'll tell you what, one simple little five-letter word, p-u-r-s-e purse.

Take the same situation, only now you're standing outside the changing room holding "the purse." I don't care who you are, how secure you think you might be in your manhood, it changes the way you feel when you hold "the purse." You go from being confident, secure, and talkative to passive, shy, and avoidant. No matter how cool you think you are, you just cannot keep your cool status when you're holding "the purse." Do you think it is by accident they take the smallest, cutest, daintiest one when you go shopping together? Of course not. They know that at some point you will be holding it, and they want you to have "the feeling." "The feeling" goes hand in hand with "the purse." What it is designed to do, is put you in your place. Just when you feel as if you're on top of the world, that nothing or no one could bring you down. When you feel as if you could take on anything or anyone. When there is no situation that would dare think of not being conquered by you. They quickly remind you they can destroy that confidence and those feelings ... with a little purse.

It's all part of the game, the dance, the control. Language takes on new meanings when we tweak it just a little bit. Doubling up words takes on whole new meanings. Code words convey real meanings. Psychological measures are used to take control of our thoughts, our ideas, and even our understanding of our very existence. All of it is done just to keep us in their grips (and, of course, to give them something to laugh at). Based upon these revelations, I have just one thing to say to you concerning this chapter.

If you thought this chapter was good, then was it really good or good, good? Whatever the hell that means. If you thought this chapter was bad, then we'll just call it good.

Chapter 4
The Toilet Seat Test

I know what you're thinking. The guys are rolling their eyes and mumbling, "Okay, this is the chapter where he's going to give it to us." Gals, on the other hand, are thinking, "YEA! WE'ARE READY TO GIVE IT TO THEM NOW!"

You're both wrong. (Yes, even the women.) This chapter is designed to develop a sense of PERSPECTIVE.

Perspective gives us clarity in a situation. Perspective is often the one thing that helps us to understand another's feelings, to have compassion for another's thoughts and experiences. Perspective is usually the one thing we, as human beings, do not have.

Take the toilet seat. As you and I both know, us men get a lot of flak for leaving the toilet seat in the UP position. Of course, we should be shot for this, so thank you for allowing us to live for all these years. This insensitive, uncaring, outrageous behavior has defined us as a gender. However, I propose a test that requires much concentration and discipline on the part of the man. Yes, I said concentration and discipline, so ninety percent of us are out. Just move on to Chapter Five. If you think you might be in the ten percent who can handle this project, then by all means keep reading. You might want to just focus on one word, though, either concentration or discipline.

Go stand in front of your toilet. Put the toilet seat down. Don't worry, guys, this isn't some kind of trick. And women, I am not on your side. When I say put the toilet seat down, I don't just mean put the toilet seat down, I mean put BOTH seats down. Yes, I said both seats. I actually implemented this test years ago, and every single time after the ladies are done, they leave that second lid up. So what does this mean?

I gathered my research and, sure enough, 100% of the time the second lid was left up during the test. After compiling the information, I then started surveying, which was the least fun part of my job. Partly because of the opening question: "Why in the world did you leave the seat up when you were done?" Universally, women didn't like this question, and I was unpopular for a while. Nevertheless, the repeated answer was something like, "Why the hell would I put it down, when all I'm going to need to do is lift it back up again the next time?"

Hallelujah, Amen, and Praise the Lord! This is what we as men have been saying for all this time. Leaving the lid up makes sense. It doesn't measure your sensitivity, your compassion, or anything else. It makes sense; it's convenient and efficient. The truly ironic thing is that now I'm simply in the habit of putting both seats down. For some strange reason, I often get upset when the seats are left up – go figure!

Okay, now you see my point. There are things that guys can do that will help get our point across. But no matter what we do, we never really win. We should be used to that, not winning, that is.

For example, we men must shave our faces. I don't know about all of you guys out there, but I will occasionally mix up my appearance. Sometimes I'm clean-shaven, sometimes I have a beard, sometimes I'll shave my eyebrows, you just never know (that last part was a joke). Whenever I keep a beard, it occasionally has to be trimmed. I say occasionally; if it was up to my wife, I would be trimming it every day (only I would be trimming it with a razor). The only problem is, when you trim a beard, it leaves a few hairs in the sink. I once saw a commercial for a trimmer that actually vacuums while you trim. I don't remember who manufactured it, but I thought it was an ingenious invention. I'm amazed it hasn't showed up under the Christmas tree. Anyway, back to my point. I usually try to clean up a little bit after I finish trimming. I do admit that it's not especially nice to have a multitude of short pieces of hair lying around the sink. However, I didn't know it was necessary to have microscopic vision and a degree in "cleanest sink in the world" just to be allowed to have a beard.

I pride myself on having 15/20 vision. I'll be the first to admit that the older I get, the more these numbers are probably changing. But I can still see. When I finish cleaning the sink, there isn't a hair left in sight. This can mean only one of two things, I am either losing my mind (which I'm not ruling out), or my wife likes to go in after I'm done and sprinkle little bits of hair on the sink. Why would she do this, you ask? Possibly to make me lose my mind, but that's a whole other topic. No, this way she can call me into the bathroom and show me hairs that I know were on a "hair free" sink. I, of course, am not allowed to clean them up because I have obviously proven that I'm not capable or competent enough to handle this task. So she does it, and then gets the opportunity to remind me that she did it the rest of the day. I am at her mercy for whatever she wants (personally I think she has a "jar" of hair that she scatters around as she sees fit). It is for this reason that I make sure I don't trim my beard on the weekend. There are more "expendable" hours in a weekend day than in a work day.

I think maybe what she does is scan with the light she uses to put on her makeup. With this light on, not only can you see hairs on the sink, but you can see atoms. I'm not kidding. What is the deal with that anyway? Nobody is trying to land a plane. I'll bet if women didn't wear makeup, utility bills would drop 85 percent. I turned it on once and it took three days for my eyes to dilate from a pinprick! She has obviously adapted to the high voltage runway path because sure enough, she goes in to put on that makeup, the light comes on, and three-and-a-half hours later she's out and ready to go.

Relativity

While on the general topic of perspective, let's address another important term. Relativity. I adopted the notion over the years that everything is relative. This is a good thing to know because I can then explain to my wife that no matter how badly I may have messed up on something, there is always another man out there who messed up something WAY worse than me. It is amazing, though, how much she doesn't care. Yet, for some reason, I keep trying to use this rationale. (I'm not sure, but this may be Webster's definition of stupid. I just hope that they got my good side with my picture that accompanies it). To show her how well it can work, I use the rationale with my wife. Sure she messes up on things occasionally, but that's relative! I'm sure there is someone's wife or girlfriend out there who messed up worse. This is the reason, and the only reason, that I may share any shortcomings of my wife with my male friends.

Men like to try and "out do" each other. I use this bit of knowledge to help build a "relativity" scale within my own relationship. All I have to do is get the ball rolling, and I am sure to hear about how someone has it worse. In a meeting the other week, I mentioned to an attendee that my wife spends so much money at Hobby Lobby that I wish they would go public so that I could buy some stock in it (I would at least get some of my money back). This attendee proceeded to tell me that with his wife, they have officially added Hobby Lobby as an expense column to the family budget, right below food and water.

This provides great comfort to me. Now I don't think that my house is not made of glass. When I mention my wife's shortcomings, this is only natural. None of us are perfect. I am aware that I have shortcomings as well. I am also aware that I may, just may, have slightly more shortcomings than my wife does (just ask her). If her shortcomings were a two-year old pine tree, mine would be a towering Redwood in a centuries old California forest. Fortunately, I have been blessed with the ability to recognize and point out the shortcomings of others. For how else would they know they needed areas of improvement?

The flip side of this works for women as well. When women congregate, they like to "out do" each other too. The only difference is they like to challenge each other as to whose man is most stupid. I still haven't figured out why it is beneficial to win this argument. Maybe you get the most sympathy? It's a moot point anyway. Comparing men and their intelligence levels is like comparing the intelligence of an armchair to that of a rock. That is, of course, measuring their intelligence to what women think is important. Most men are not aware of the latest fall fashions, which celebrities are dating, and how many kids Brad Pitt has. This certainly does not monopolize women's focus, but this news does earn more attention in most women compared to most men. There are just differences in interest and knowledge. My argument is that lack of this knowledge does not make us stupid. My wife asked me to pick up some things at the fabric store one time, and couldn't understand why it took me three hours. I decided to send my wife to the automotive store to pick up a few things, and she hasn't sent me to the fabric store since.

I remember taking a psychology course in college. It was amazing to me to learn how people and the human brain work. I remember one study in particular that consisted of a control group, and the task was simply to look at two lines and determine which was longer. We'll call them line A and line B.

Now clearly line A is longer than line B. In this particular study though, the control group was to say that line B is the longer of the two. The control group consisted of everyone in the study except for one person. The one person was the only one who could look at the two lines and make an objective decision as to which was longer. After twenty-five people finished saying line B was longer, the one independent variable was basically forced to agree. Pretty sneaky, huh? Our need to conform can sometimes outweigh our ability to make a rationale judgment. If you're a woman then this is no news to you.

Women have been using this strategy for quite some time. They don't really care if they conform with each other; they are more interested in conforming the men. This is why they always want to "change" the man they are with. Now for a long time this was something I didn't understand. Why would you get to know someone, find things you like about them, start a relationship with them, and then try to "change" them? One of the main reasons I came up with goes back to them trying to make us lose our minds. But I believe that this is just an added bonus. I think the real reason they try to change us is to make us all the same. Take a wedding, for example. Here we have a ceremony representing the unification of these two people who fell in love and are ready to commit a life of everlasting happiness together. Women pay attention to every detail – the flowers, the cake, the napkins, location, guests, dresses, and a tux. Why is it that the napkins and the photographer's suit have to match perfectly, but every man in any wedding party is dressed like a penguin?

I'll tell you why. It is the ultimate showcase of how the woman has "changed" him. It is as if she is saying to everyone, "Look, here he is. He used to be an individual, one with individual ideas, thoughts and opinions, but I have successfully 'changed' all that. He is no longer 'him,' he is 'them,' and you may now do with him, I mean them, as you please. He can no longer think for himself, so you may now do all the thinking for him. He is ready to join in the ranks of all the others who came before him, who thought they, too, could survive on their own. Foolish, foolish man, what were you possibly thinking? Did you really think you could be different and survive our clutches?"

Now this may be troubling to read if you're a man, but don't worry. If you're in a relationship, just go home and ask your significant other if this is true. She will surely let you know that it is not, and you can continue comfortably about your life. (Ignorance is bliss.)

"Sex (now do I have your attention)"

I don't think it is any big secret as to how women have this control over us, right? It is because of our need to be in a loving, caring relationship with the potential for growth and synergy over the years to come; in other words, sex! Yes, women have always had power over us because of sex. We want it, and they can give it to us. I once remember hearing that men think about sex something like 132 times every five minutes. My only question is what about the other 168 seconds? Yes, this source of control is what clearly lets me know that God is a woman, and oh, what fun is She having.

We men will do just about anything for sex. Rationality gets thrown right out the window. We'll spend countless hours and an enumerable amount of energy on just the possibility we may have sex. If women didn't know this, then it really wouldn't be a problem. However, women do know this. Even though they would *never* use it as a manipulative tool to get what they want. . . okay, I'll stop that sentence there. They are still human beings who are unable to *avoid using* this to their advantage. So here lies man's (and I mean "man" in the literal term, not mankind) greatest weakness. Yes, we've tried many things to overcome this weakness, from masturbation to blow up dolls to homosexuality, but none of them have helped. I guess we'll just continue to give in. However, I will offer these tips on things that you can do to stack the deck in your favor. Remember to extend the same courtesy and *never* use this as a manipulative tool…...

Sex Tips

Tip # 1: Whatever she wants you to do, in the words of Nike, Just Do It! I know, it defies the whole control factor. The good news is, more than likely, you will get the sex! Now I know you think you're in control of the relationship, that you can get it whenever you want! All I can say is young, young fool! It is obvious you have either just started dating or have been in one short-lived relationship after another. Try dating a woman for more than eighteen days, then talk to me. Women will typically let you be fooled for a little while, then just when you've eliminated your other options they drop the hammer on you. I won't even go into the multitude of excuses (I mean reasons), but let's just say they are plenty. Just do what she wants, and hope for the best.

Tip # 2: Whatever she wants you to do, in the words of Nike, Just Do It! – I can't stress this enough, so I thought it was worth mentioning again.

Tip # 3: First Things First! Dr. Stephen Covey describes this as Habit 3 in *The Seven Habits of Highly Effective People* I'm putting it as Tip 3 in "The Seven Things I Would Do Just to Have Sex." Dr. Covey discusses the importance of identifying the most important and "attention" needed items in your life, and then appropriately prioritizing and addressing those items. What I am suggesting is no different: put her needs before yours.

A simple scenario illustrates this. I think it could be agreed upon that, for the most part, women are compassionate beings. Keeping that in mind, if we men put their needs first, then they are almost compelled on some level to address our needs. This is a plus for us, a win/win scenario (another one of Dr. Covey's philosophies). Now let's address the flip side of this. Let's say we put our needs first. Think about this real hard. Our needs have been met. Are we men compassionate enough to meet her needs at this point? I've tried to survey this, but the women said they could never wake the men up in order to get an answer! Yes, if we put her needs first, then we are sure to have our needs met. If we put our needs first, then that is where I believe the phrase "cold day in Hell" originated from.

Tip # 4: Alcohol! I don't know why, it just works.

Tip # 5: Don't date a woman for more than eighteen days! I touched on this earlier. If you want to keep thinking you're a stud and in control of your relationships and the "sex availability" factor, then by all means keep doing what you're doing. Just keep in mind that some day, all the women are going to find someone they can manipulate, change, put a tuxedo on, and then you are left with masturbation, blow up dolls, or homosexuality. So be careful and weigh your options.

Tip # 6: Get Rich! And by rich I mean lots of money. This is, of course, an area that I had to survey, because I don't have lots of money, but it works. Don't ask me why it works, it just does. It must address some primal level of "being taken care of" or something like that. A word of caution though. Someone will always have more money, and you know what that means. They then get the sex, and leave you with one of two options. 1. Find someone else you can impress with the "money" life, or 2. Masturbation, blow up dolls or homosexuality. Funny how this keeps coming up?

Tip # 7: Pray genetics are good to you. Yes, any woman who says that size doesn't matter is lying to you. It does. That shouldn't come as a surprise. If you're hungry, do you want a cracker or a meal?

The same goes for women. They'll settle for a cracker, but they usually don't have to. In fact, if size is not your thing, I suggest you pay special attention to Tip # 6. Does this mean there's no hope for you if you're not rich or genetically gifted? Absolutely not, just keep in mind that your "chances for success" are marginal. You may be left with masturbation . . . (I don't really need to list all three again, do I?)

Tip # 8: Hang out with ugly people. I know it sounds bad, but it makes sense if you really think about it. Guys, say you're out at the club and you happen to be paying attention to the female clientele. A group of this female clientele comes up to you while at the club. The first thing you do is pick out the most attractive one. It's human nature, so take advantage of it. Women do it, too, so it's okay. Go find the ugliest friends you can, and your chances of sex will increase, I guarantee it.

Tip # 9: Don't be selective. Have sex with whoever will give it to you. Believe it or not, there are plenty of women out there who go through dry spells. Just go with the flow and don't be too selective. This will certainly ramp up your sex life.

Tip # 10: Be careful with Tip # 9. Actually I don't really recommend Tip # 9 at all; it's just asking for trouble.

So let's review. These tips may not improve the "quality" of your sex life, but the list is for men so we're addressing "quantity" here. (Women, I would tell you that now that you have this list you know what to look out for. However, I know you already know, so it's kind of a moot point.)

1. *Just Do It*
2. *Just Do It*
3. *First Things First*
4. *Alcohol*
5. *Don't date a woman more than 18 days*
6. *Get Rich*
7. *Pray that genetics is good to you*

44

> 8. *Hang out with ugly people*
> 9. *Don't be selective*
> 10. *Be careful with tip # 9*

Yes, all these things can help. They can help on an individual level, or you can combine tips to increase your chances even more. For example, combine tip *# 4 Alcohol* with any of them and you've automatically more than doubled your chances. So men, study this list, and I hope that it will help your sex life improve.

The Variable Factor

The variable factor is another tool women use to help keep men in control. It's subtle, so it can be hard to pick up on. It is almost mathematical in nature, so I debated about putting it in Chapter Two: Female Mathematics. I think, though, that it fits better here.

It always seems like a major accomplishment when we as men do something "right" for our women. It's especially nice when that "something right" is done as an unselfish act that wasn't asked for. Now, women do this for men all the time, and they make it seem so effortless. Women imply that it isn't a difficult task. Or is it?

This variable factor was finally made evident to me one morning when my wife and I were about to have breakfast. It was a simple morning, just a bowl of cereal. Yet this seemingly simple task can be made quite complicated. Fixing my cereal required only a few things, a bowl, a spoon, cereal and milk. In fact, I went to college so I have gotten by on this scenario with far less, but we'll stick with these items for now. Fixing her cereal was a far more complicated process. She got out a bowl, a spoon, two different kinds of cereal (of the four in the cabinet), a measuring cup, some fruit from the freezer (of the twelve), and milk. So let's say she was going to fix my cereal for me that morning. She could pour my box of cereal (of the *one* in the cabinet) into the bowl, pour in some milk, and then insert spoon. Very easy process, wouldn't you agree? There were only four variables, and they fit in a very logical order. Say she asks me to fix her cereal. Well, I have to figure out which two of the four boxes of cereal she wants to have fixed *that* morning.

Then I have to figure out how much of each one to pour into the bowl. This may be where the measuring cup comes in, but I think it is only used for one of the cereals. Already my chances for success are pretty low. Then I have to figure out which frozen fruit to put in with the cereal. I am dead now for sure. Then, let's just say that I got all this correct (fat chance). I have to figure out how much milk to put in the cereal (I think the measuring cup is used here again). If you happen to get all this right, she'll just tell you that you gave her the wrong spoon.

You see how it is impossible to get things correct? Even if it was exactly what they wanted, they can lie and say it wasn't and you have to believe them because of the Variable Factor (and we also already discussed this in Chapter 1: In The Beginning). Women will try to explain their actions with diet or something like that, but I personally am not falling for it any more. I have said it before: Men are simple creatures. Sometimes this works to our advantage; in this situation it does not. Women simply use the Variable Factor as a means of control. It occurs in too many situations to just be tied to diet, but let's just get the obvious "diet" ones out of the way first.

I drink my coffee two ways, hot and black. Pretty simple. Kind of hard to mess it up. My wife drinks her coffee pretty simple as well, the right way and the wrong way. She doesn't go overboard with the Variable Factor in this sense; she could certainly use sugar, sweeteners, or some kind of flavorful coffee additive. No, she just adds either milk or crème. If I put milk in, she wanted crème. If I put crème in, you get the idea. Now I know some of you men think you're smart, and you're going to *ask* her what she wants. Her response, of course, to you is "shouldn't you know what I want by now?" Don't ever ask, guys. Just accept the fact that you're going to have it wrong.

Let's move the scenarios to the public sector, restaurants. Could someone please tell me why in the hell restaurants have menus? I mean, it sounds like a crazy concept to me that an establishment would have a combination of different entrees that come with a group of sides to best match those entrees. Okay, actually I think this sounds like a pretty good idea. I mean, you tell me what goes good together, and I'll figure out which steak I want.

This process isn't quite as simple for women. Women always want to change things around on the menu. Any change that requires the calling in of a mathematician isn't worth it. Again, women will try to use the "diet" excuse for this one as well. Don't fall for it. If it was truly for diet reasons, then why in the world would she go to use the restroom just as the waiter is coming (you, of course, don't see him coming), and ask you to order for her. She'll just have the salmon. BOOM, Variable Factor! The only thing that you can safely assume at this point is that whatever combination of foods listed with the salmon, is not the right combination. You are forced to make a decision and if *you're really* paying attention, then you did not ask her what combination she wanted before she left. The good news is that now you can just relax and know that she owns the rest of the evening. You should have pretty much known this anyway because you already messed up on the drink order.

When we go out and if we have a drink, it's pretty much always the same with me – I'll have a beer please. I may try to order a specific kind of beer, but if I leave to go to the restroom and I come back and have a beer waiting on me, PERFECT! I don't really give a damn what kind of beer it is as long as it's cold, and even that isn't critical. My wife doesn't like beer, so at least I know I can count that out of the Variable Factor. However, you can quickly see, that even if there are only *two* drinks that she likes, I am destined to get the wrong one.

Variable Factor: Clothing and Organization

You can be sure I don't even try to recommend any type of clothing combination. This is clear proof, though, that the Variable Factor is not exclusive to dieting scenarios. If so, then we wouldn't even be addressing this.

If you really look at the situation, it goes much deeper than styles and colors. I've gone shopping with my wife before, and I have yet to see one line of clothing whose size is consistent with other lines. I mean, what the hell are women talking about when they either say "I am a size two" or, "I could never fit into a size two"? Both of these could be true (no matter what size you are) if you just shop around long enough.

The same is true for decorating. Fortunately, my wife and I have similar taste. I swear though that I looked at a wall of three million colors, and two million of them were the same. I think the paint manufacturers just like to mess with us. If you have a yellow color named "sunshine," there is no need to add one more drop of a brighter color and call it "golden sunshine", or to add one more drop of a slightly darker color and call it "sunshine in Seattle." What the hell ever happened to calling yellow "yellow" anyway? I guess if we were sent to the store to buy "yellow" paint and we came back with "yellow" paint, then that would be too simple, huh? I went to the paint store, and let me tell you what "yellow" is now called. I found bright star, bright sunshine, sunny summer, summer sunflower, citrus splash, neon light, lemon tart, iced lemon, lemon drops, marigold, pineapple soda, yellow brick road, empire yellow, daffodil yellow, bumblebee yellow, joyful yellow, eastern colonial yellow, vintage scotch yellow, and hello yellow. I'm serious. You can't make this stuff up. Now at least if all these finely named colors *looked* different, then I could maybe understand the need for colorful names (pun intended), but they are all just yellow.

Along with clothing and decorating comes the "organization" of items within the home. Organization is a "relative" word here, so were going to play with it a bit. My wife and I have a little game we play. It's called "I picked this beautiful item up from the store because it is magnificent and I can't live without it, only I don't know what the hell to do with it so you find a place for it." I'm the one who gets to find "a place." To be honest with you, this relationship works out pretty well. Fortunately, I usually like what she brings home, and she usually likes where I put it. But……this is not *always* the case. For example, we were both shopping in an antique store one day and she saw this little box for storing things in what looks like a book. She showed it to me, and the price was reasonable so we decided to get it. I found a place for it at home on a small bench near our front door. I thought it would be a good place to drop the keys in when we came home (Lord only knows what's in there now and I don't dare put my keys in there for fear that it might take me three days to find them).

Anyway, I put the box there and we both seemed to like it. I did notice the next day, though, that somebody must have bumped it because it was now a little crooked. No big deal, I just straightened it out and went on with my day. Until the next day when I noticed it was crooked again. So I straightened it up and went about my day.

Well, this little process went on for about two weeks before I finally wondered what in the hell could possibly be going on. Come to find out, my wife likes things at an "angle" as opposed to straight (the way it should be). I know what an angle is, and as far as I am concerned there is only one appropriate one and that is 90 degrees. She doesn't see it this way. In fact, as I type these words, I am sitting at our "angled" bar, next to our "angled" bookshelf, across from our "angled" couch. Of course, our antique box is at an "angle" to this day as well. It's okay though, I just pretend that North is 45 degrees clockwise from where it really is and it always works out. Wait a minute. Doesn't the axis of the earth sit on an angle? See, God really is a woman.

So with the Variable Factor you can clearly see that we men don't have a chance. Our only way to get things right is if women "decide" it is right. Don't blame us for continuing to try; most of us haven't even figured out that we can't win. As I've said, I'm convinced it is a plot against us. I know that fixing a cup of coffee is like handing over a hammer and waiting to see if I'll be struck by it or not. I also know that no matter what number is printed on that tag underneath that four-letter word S I Z E, I am doomed. How could you think I was a size ____ (insert any number here, it doesn't really matter)? If the number is too low, then she'll say you wish she were smaller. If the number is too high, then she'll say you think she is too big. And if she ever says to you "does this make me look fat" then bite your tongue until you draw blood if you have to. Whatever you do, DO NOT ANSWER! It is another "no win situation." I will go more into this in the next Chapter – "Wait before you comment on weight."

Chapter 5
Wait Before You Comment on Weight

It should be no surprise the title of this chapter should be taken quite literally. Women will always try to rope men into their circle of control by asking one of a series of questions. If you as a man have ever been in a relationship for more than two and a half seconds, you're familiar with the questions. They will be something like "Does this make my butt look big" or "Does this make me look fat?" Or how about "Is she prettier than me?" Women do this for one simple reason: it is a test.

I don't know why we're always being tested, but we are. I thought when I was done with college I would be finished with the tests. Boy, was I wrong. In hindsight, all my years of testing in school were probably practice for the "woman tests," and in my opinion, I don't think I was adequately prepared. Maybe you have to get a master's degree?

I remember in grade school we were given a standardized test called the Iowa Basics. I don't think they have them anymore; we've evolved to a much more enlightened society now and focus more on "individuality" and less on "standardization." Anyway, I was thinking, wouldn't it be cool if they gave a standardized test on how to deal with some of the questions and situations that women present us?

Wait a minute, I think I have it! Okay, pay attention here. If you're a man, you'll really want to pay attention. The answer to all the previous questions is NO! I know this seems like a very simple concept, but men are easily fooled when asked these questions because we think it is some form of test. Remember when we talked about man's inability to lie? This is what seems like a test for us. We feel they are testing us to see if we'll say what we want them to hear, even if it might be a lie. Of course, if we lie in this situation, then we're clearly comfortable to do it in any other situation. This means they need to keep an eye on us to make sure we don't lie in other situations. We have already learned, however, that men cannot effectively do this anyway, so I don't know why they bother with the test.

Despite the fact that it may indeed be a lie, go ahead and say "NO" anyway. The consequences of lying are far less than a "YES" answer, or even a slight hesitation for that matter. The truth of the matter is they want you to lie right now. By all means, give them what they want.

It's ridiculous to ask such a subjective question anyway. I have never understood this. Again, I'm no doctor, but it is my opinion that one should be at a weight that is comfortable to them. We're all made up differently; we have different lifestyles, different genetics. We are not all meant to look the same. I myself am a rather small guy, and always have been. In my high school and early college years, I worked very hard at gaining weight. At one point I was on a routine schedule of taking weight gainer, creatine, and protein whey. I did this in combination with a heavy lifting schedule. The result: I didn't change a pound. I know this concept sickens most people, and that it would also sicken most people that I weigh the same now that I did when I graduated high school in 1991. The point is, however, that I have finally come to accept that this is the weight I am, and I am comfortable with it. More important to me is that I keep as healthy as possible.

The subjectivity of weight is an interesting study in and of itself. I remember studying something about this during a psychology course in college. If my memory serves me correctly, there is a distinct difference between what women thought men wanted in a size, and what men thought women wanted in a size. Let's produce a model here, and we'll just call it the *"psychological scale."* Now let's create a framework of comparison here, and create a scale with two extreme differences in weight. On one side of the model we'll have a "supermodel," and on the other side of the model we'll have "Jabba the Hutt."

•────────────────────────────────────•
   Supermodel   Jabba the Hutt

All women fit on this model somewhere. The only real certainty with this model is that no matter where a woman may fit on it, it is guaranteed that she would like to be one millimeter closer to the Supermodel side (unless she is already a Supermodel in which two other things are guaranteed. 1. Obviously she is perfectly happy with everything in her life, and 2. I don't know her). If you know any women at all, then you've already realized the absurdity of this model. The problem lies in the fact that if a woman moves one millimeter toward the Supermodel side – she still wants to move one millimeter toward the Supermodel side. How absurd is that? I mean, take some time to enjoy an accomplishment! Realize you met a goal! Reward yourself mentally and spiritually! But no, "I just have one more millimeter to go" is all we ever hear.

Okay, so the previous millimeter comment may be a slight extreme (and I do mean slight). Most women are reasonable and understand we can't all be Supermodels, and set a modest and realistic goal for their weight. The funny thing is, women try to set a range they think men like. This is when the psychological aspects of weight get interesting, and when the "psychological scale" comes into play. What we are going to look at first here is where women think men want to see them on the psychological scale. We will indicate the mark with a vertical segment (I'd say line but lines never end, that was geometry, not psychology).

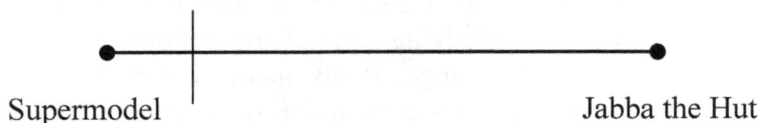

Supermodel   Jabba the Hut

Being rational and reasonable, women know this line is about the closest they can get to being perfect (after all, only Supermodels are perfect, and they were just born that way). This line, I mean segment (sorry, Mrs. Wurtz) represents the reasonable "optimal" weight for most women. This, of course, being based upon what men like and want. The interesting thing about the study of psychology was that when men were asked where they thought the optimal weight was for women, their answer was a little bit different. The dotted line (okay, if I use the words "line" and "segment" interchangeably, just know what I mean) represents where women think men want them to be on the weight scale. The solid line represents where men actually want women. It looks something like this.

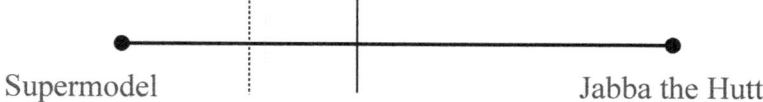

The interesting thing was that men tended to prefer sizes a little farther away from the Supermodel size than women had suspected. This really made sense to me because if I would ever bump into a Supermodel, I think the first thing I would do is try to buy her a hamburger. It is rather peculiar, however, that women think this is what we men want.

When I say *want*, it's important to understand something here. If a fashion show is on, and there are Supermodels pacing back and forth on the catwalk, don't ask us "is that what you want?" The reason why you shouldn't ask us that is because you may get unspecified feedback. If a woman asks that question, she is probably asking based on some sort of "psychological scale" in an effort to assess what size we really like. The problem is if you ask us if that is what we want, and we say *no*, then you're going to know that we're lying. But we are answering a different question. We don't understand that you're evaluating our response to subject yourself as an ultimate competitor on the psychological scale. We are just answering "is that what you want" in which case, no matter what we say verbally, we are thinking "sure, I'll take some of that."

We're not really answering the question that women are asking. We are men, we like women, we want them all the time, we can't help our desire. Honestly, if Jabba the Hutt had bigger breasts and some lipstick and you asked the same question, we would say no, but try to tell if we are lying.

The psychological scale for men is a little bit different. Man has decided he knows what women like, and we work hard to get there. This includes going to the gym for many hours a week, working on getting nice and bulked up. Yes, we men know what women want is the Incredible Hulk, just maybe a little better-tempered and a little less "reactive" looking. We work hard at this so we can be on the proper side of the scale. Let's take a look at where men think that they are supposed to be at on the psychological scale.

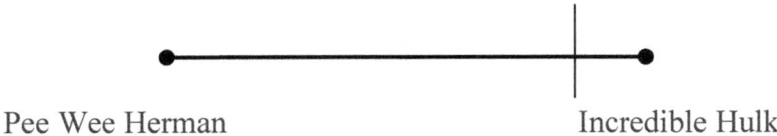

Pee Wee Herman   Incredible Hulk

The difference between men and women is most women know they will never reach the Supermodel range. Men, however, actually think they can bulk up to their desired size. The way to do this, of course, is to figure out how much weight you can possibly lift in any and every exercise, then put ten more pounds on than that when you work out (that is unless a good looking woman comes into the room, then you put one thousand more pounds). The result is the same no matter how much more weight you put on. You try to lift it, you can't, so you scream, holler, then hold your breath, turn red, have an aneurysm, and then say out loud that you must be off today. After you do this so everyone in the gym has had a chance to see it, you go stand in front of the mirror and admire how much bigger you've gotten from your strenuous workout.

Of course, you are now not able to walk or move the next day because, after all, there were a lot of people in the gym so you worked out more than usual. This inability to move is the only thing keeping you from becoming the Incredible Hulk. You'll get back at it as soon as the doctor says it's okay. In the meantime, we will have to settle with being a "mediocre" hulk. The funny thing is, if we look at where women would prefer men to be on the scale of weight, we get a slightly different picture. Again, we will indicate the previous perception (man's perception) with a dotted line, and women's preference with a solid line.

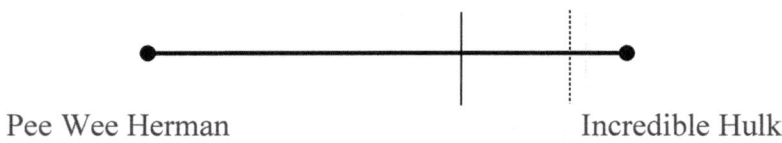

Pee Wee Herman   Incredible Hulk

As you can see, men and women both seem to have a skewed perception about where the other sex would like to see them on the weight scale. As near as I can tell, it seems that each sex is actually trying to create in themselves, to some degree, what they would like to see in the other. I don't mean to suggest that men want their women to look like the Incredible Hulk, but I do suggest that men would like to see their women a little heavier than what women think. On the same token, surely women don't want their men to look (or act) like Pee Wee Herman (especially act, and I'm not referring to his acting ability, but rather his public performances). But we find that women tend to prefer us men a little smaller than we may think. I think the only ones who have a true grasp on what their partner wants are the homosexuals. They are the only ones who, based on this psychological scale, truly understand what their partners want.

The important thing, of course, is that we are healthy. In America, we are all about the health. Just take a watch at the television set some evening (and by evening, I mean insomniac time). The television set is filled with different pills, remedies, and workout equipment to help us get "healthy." And thank goodness, too, because without these products, none of us could go to "this." We would constantly be stuck at "this." Fortunately, with these products, we can go from this to this (just imagine that there was some cheesy music and that the page blurred for a second, then when you came back the page was suddenly ripped. Oh, I mean ripped as in cut, wait a minute that doesn't work either, okay just imagine when you came back that the writing was actually good! There, that works.).

Yes, these products can magically transform us into what each sex wants for themselves in the other sex, and often in as little as seven minutes a day. Boy, how wonderful are these things. To just be able to drink this drink and look like them, it's just great to be alive in these times. Or to do just two and a half crunches on this particular machine, and get the same result as if I'd done five hundred or a thousand, I mean that's fantastic. And the people they show that it has worked for? It's like they were sent from the heavens above. Perfectly sculpted into exactly what we think the other sex wants.

If you haven't been able to tell, you should be detecting just a little bit of sarcasm here. What kind of world do we live in when marketers toy with the weaknesses of other's emotions just to make a few bucks? And oftentimes, all for the sake of health. Here's a healthy idea, turn the television off at two o'clock in the morning and go to sleep. It's just sad, I tell you! What is most frightening is how many people actually fall for the concept. If I get this, I'll look like that! I mean, let's evaluate what they advertised to us. First of all, I don't need a lot of space. This device will easily set up in the smallest corner of my house. It provides the maximum workout in the smallest space. Most importantly, when I'm not using it, I can conveniently break it down and store it under my bed, or even in my jacket pocket if I desire.

What's really important to understand here, though, is how easy it is to put this device together, and how easy it is to take apart. I've built things I bought (I'm talking about a bookshelf or something – not this workout equipment), and I'll admit that it sometimes is quite frustrating. It will look simple enough, but then turns out to be quite challenging. My process usually goes something like this. I open everything up in the middle of the living room, so my wife can see the challenge I have before me (also the TV is in there). Then I set the directions to the side and start away. There are two very important things to keep in mind when undertaking such a project. The first is don't actually throw the directions away. The second is to always look like you know what you're doing.

The first of these two things should be obvious. You're going to need the directions later (and by later, I mean at some point when no woman is in the room). The second of these two things is oftentimes the most difficult. It would be okay if we were never *asked* what we were doing, but women know we don't know what the hell we are doing, so they can't help but test us. The situation usually goes something like this.

Woman: What are you doing?

Incompetent man pretending to be competent: I'm building this bookshelf.

Woman: No, I mean right now. What are you doing right now, and what is that piece you're holding?

Man thinking quickly and also looking to see what he has in his hand: Well, this is the flux capacitor and I am holding it so that it can finish balancing before I insert it into the hyperdrive (marked "C") then I'll be almost done.

Woman: Whatever.

The only thing the man can count on at this point is that the woman doesn't like the same movies he does and she hopefully bought it. Now he says he's almost done, but he knows, she knows, hell even the bookshelf knows, that this is far from the truth. This is just an attempt to ward off more questions.

This type of frustration is why it's important for marketers to show the ease of assembling and un-assembling a piece of workout equipment. Of course, I mean the ease of assembling and un-assembling "their" piece of workout equipment. The competitor's equipment is another story. The competitors have a piece of equipment that does half the stuff, is twice as big, is hard to handle, and costs double. The advertiser will show the difficulty some people have with their competitor's equipment, featuring them holding part of the equipment and physically show an exaggerated level of frustration. This frustration level can only be described as trying to insert a square peg into a round hole. The bedraggled, sweating person eventually gives up, and we see a beautiful person showing the ease of getting ready to use "their" equipment.

This ease is important because women see this and think that even their husbands could put this together. We know this is far from the truth. What I wish they would do though is show what *really* happens when someone gets frustrated assembling something. A five-second attempt with a casual, but exaggerated "give up" head shake is far from an accurate depiction of reality.

I have to tell you, I have gotten a square peg into a round hole before. It wasn't pretty mind you, but I got it. That is what I would do with this piece of workout equipment. You don't want to fold up for storage? I'll fold you up for storage! The problem is trying to fold it up using the tools that were sent with it. I go and get the universal tool, either Mr. Hammer or his older brother Sledge. I find these tools can do just about anything. So could we please see someone invoking this process in the commercial? It would at least be more believable.

Falling for this gimmick is a little bit understandable, but I would have to ask myself one question before every purchase. For example, let's say there is an advertisement for an abdominal machine. The advertisement talks about how this machine isolates the abdominal muscles and cuts your workout time in half. My first question would be, "What is my current workout time?" If my current workout time is *zero*, then half of zero is zero. It is unreasonable to assume that a new piece of workout equipment will guarantee a sustained workout schedule. This is where we get hooked, and where we absolve the maker of the equipment of responsibility of lack of results.

My wife has been asking for a treadmill for some time now. When the weather is nice, she runs outside. When the weather is bad, she uses the treadmill at the hospital where she works. We just bought a treadmill. I'm confident it will get some use. This type of purchase I am fine with, and I do believe a lot of the reason has to do with health. Sure, it can help keep the pounds off, too, but it's not a "get fit quick" attempt.

Speaking of getting fit, I have a new Zen riddle that needs to be added to the books. By Zen riddle I am, of course, referring to such philosophical questions as "if a tree falls in the forest and there is no one around to here it, does it make a sound?" Or how about "what is the sound of one hand clapping?" Here is my one to add to the books: "I have to get in shape before going to the gym." What? I don't understand this concept at all. This concept is solely owned by the women, not the men. I have never heard a man speak this utter nonsense. I would like to be able to offer an answer to this, but I guess it's unanswerable. For women, this must somehow make sense because they all do it. If a man were to say this, it would clearly be an excuse to not go workout. Women will actually go get in shape before starting a workout routine at a gym. Some things just aren't meant to be understood.

If a woman says she needs to get in shape, don't agree or disagree. Just keep your mouth shut. If she asks if she looks fat, keep your mouth shut. If she asks if her friend looks pretty, keep your

mouth shut. In fact, anything that has to do with weight or appearance, just keep your mouth shut. This is probably the simplest rule for men when dealing with the woman-talk code.
    JUST KEEP YOUR MOUTH SHUT.

Chapter 6
If It Ain't Broke, Fix It

I have to start this chapter out with a story. I'd like to think this situation has only happened to me, but I'm sure there are others who can relate. Before starting, I would like to remind everybody that I have an excellent marriage, and my wife and I respect each other very much. We would never intentionally do anything we thought would be disrespectful to the other. That being said, this next story is an interesting one.

I had a unique living situation when my wife and I first met. I lived alone in a 1,660-square-foot house I purchased about a year before we met. I wouldn't exactly have called it a typical bachelor's pad; I mentioned before I'm a neat freak. It did, however, have a sense of testosterone to it. For starters, I spent a lot of my time on the main level, and my office was in the dining room. I didn't do much dining, so it worked out alright. I also didn't have too many "flowery" items around. I'll define "flowery" as those things that you find only when a woman is around. Knick-knacks, candles, curtains or window treatments, things of that sort. Probably the closest thing I came to was a couple of plants.

What made my living situation unique was that I actually bought the house I grew up in. I had gone away to college, then later moved back to the area where I was from. My parents were purchasing a new house after thirty years of being in the one I bought from them. When I moved in, there wasn't a lot of redecorating done right away. It was hard enough for my mother to see me move my office into the dining room. So for the most part, the interior decorating remained the same.

When my wife and I met (ironically at a party I had at my house), we were five months away from totally redoing the entire inside of my house. My poor mother had to deal with her first born getting married, and the house she lived in for over thirty years being totally redone. We started, one room at a time. Nothing too drastic, painting, window treatments. My mother jokes about it to this day, but the transition for her was harder than she lets on. We had pretty much remodeled every room in the house, with the exception of the kitchen. The kitchen was made up of mostly counter space and cabinetry. However, wallpaper my wife didn't care for covered a little wall space. It was next on her list. Fortunately, we share similar taste, and all the changes that had been made were mutually agreed upon, until the kitchen.

Mind you, I wasn't exactly emotionally attached to the wallpaper in the kitchen, but it wasn't bad. After all, there wasn't a lot of actual wall space anyway. But my wife, Lida, was insistent upon changing it. Since at that time she was relatively new to our great country of America, I felt it necessary to educate her on some of the common American sayings. I educated her on this one: "If it ain't broke, don't fix it."

I went to bed that night, confident the situation had at least been temporarily resolved. I wasn't naïve enough to think this comment would satisfy her forever, but I figured I bought myself at least a year. This could not have been further from the truth.

The next day I went to work. I came home to find half of one wall stripped of the wallpaper. I tried to figure out all of the logical scenarios that could have caused this. I quickly concluded there were none, so I called for my wife. "Honey, what happened to the wallpaper in the kitchen?" I asked. She came walking downstairs, took a look at it with a smirk on her face and said, "It's broke, I guess you should fix it."

As I mentioned before, my wife and I have a good relationship. There is no way that she would have done that if she didn't know that it wouldn't really bother me. Needless to say, our kitchen became a different color, camel hair, and it actually looked quite nice.

"Fixing it" is something men and women tend to do quite differently. For example, women are always trying to "fix it" when it comes to their bodies. The problem with this is that they have to fix something, even if it ain't broke. Going back to the last chapter, "Wait Before You Comment on Weight," we have learned that as men we are to keep our mouths shut. Women on the other hand have a constant battle with themselves about fixing the weight that they are. Their goal is to always fix their weight by two more pounds.

Again this concept can quickly be identified from Chapter Two, "Female Mathematics," but we will address it from the "fixing" perspective in this chapter.

Weight isn't the only thing women try to fix. Women try to fix their hair, skin, clothes, jewelry, purses, hats, homes, cars, husbands, boyfriends, girlfriends, careers, education, makeup, noses, breasts, wrinkles, just to name a few. The paradox of all of this is that no matter what the situation is, it always needs fixing. Take hair, for an example. What is the best length for hair on a woman? Answer, whatever length it currently is not. And color? You guessed it, whatever color it currently is not.

My wife went through a bit of an early midlife crisis when she was about thirty. She was in nursing school and went on an exchange student program to Ireland. She was gone for about seven weeks. When she came back I picked her up from the airport. This seemed like a simple task, but I was thrown for a bit of a loop.

I arrived at the airport exactly two minutes before her plane was scheduled to arrive. Of course, her plane was about twenty minutes early, and the other seven students who traveled with her had all already been greeted by their families. So much for "by the minute" scheduling from the airline companies. Anyway, I'm on my way to the terminal, thinking that I am two minutes early. As I get to her terminal, I walk by a very cute redhead with very short hair. She is smiling at me as I walk by her, so in effort to not be rude I smile back. Now I'll admit she was cute, so it may have been a big smile, and it may have been for a while. Oh yeah, I may have also almost walked into a door I was walking toward. I'm only human; she was cute. The only problem was, she was my wife and I didn't know it. She left for Ireland as a long-haired blonde, and came back as a short-haired redhead. She, of course, didn't tell me, which is why I got in trouble for staring at her and smiling the way I did. I explained to her that she couldn't really get mad at me, since it was actually her.

I have to admit that women are not exclusive to this concept of "if it ain't broke, fix it." No, we men are guilty as well, just in a slightly different way. What I mean is men often fix things that may not be broken; they just don't work exactly the way we want them to.

Yes, it is true. We will tear something completely apart just to get to the source of a real (or imagined) problem. What sorts of things do we tear apart? If you're married or have spent any significant time in a relationship with a man, then you know the answer is anything. Anything that can come apart, we take apart. We will even go and buy special tools to accomplish this. Of course, the reason we need to buy special tools is because some engineer decided to put a particular piece of hardware together with special fasteners to keep our dumb asses from getting into it. Have you ever seen a sticker that runs over a sealed edge of a piece of equipment that says "Warning, Warranty Voided If Sticker is Removed"? Well, that sticker is put there by the engineers because they know some dumb ass man (like myself) is going to tear into that piece of equipment like they knew what the hell they are doing. They figure if they put the sticker there, then they can eliminate about 99.99% of the issues people have with their particular product (and they would be correct). Nevertheless, we dive in with no fear whatsoever (ignorance is bliss).

Everything is fine with the process. We take calculated steps as we take stuff apart. Women may think there is nothing wrong with the particular piece of equipment that we're attacking (I mean, fixing), but they could not be further from the truth. It can certainly be either faster, stronger, bigger, heavier, louder, or any other "er" that you may see appropriate to fit here. Women are very tolerant creatures, however, so they let us make our ill-fated attempt at trying to enhance our "gadget" (plus, they know we will have to buy a new one if we don't get it put back together correctly).

Speaking of getting it put back together correctly, that is the only real flaw in our attempts at improvement. It's strange. Every step of the disassembly process seems to make perfect sense. Furthermore, we're very careful to make a mental checklist of how everything came apart, and then immediately reverse engineer it in our mind so it can go back together the same way. I don't know at what point in the process we look down at the pile of screws, bolts, wires, diodes, gears, belts, pins and/or buttons, and say out loud "holy crap," but that point does come. Our only saving grace is that the particular piece of equipment wasn't working properly anyway (by our standards), so it doesn't really matter that we can't get it put back together correctly. Thirty minutes later, you can find us at the store.

Since I started writing this book (and we're talking about a long "since" here), my wife and I have been blessed with two children, Kalvin, who just turned four (and who knows how old by the time you're actually reading this), and Klara who is two. They are nineteen months apart in age, and never leave a dull moment. I actually have just begun picking up this writing again for the first time since Kalvin was born. That's how much attention they both require and deserve. That being said, things have changed significantly in the book world since I started writing this one. For example, you may be reading a digital copy of this book, which didn't even exist when I started writing it (at least not at the ease and "commercialism" ready that it is now). The kids have certainly taken a lot away in the areas of productivity and spare time, but they are the best thing that has ever happened to us, and we now cannot imagine our lives without them.

If you haven't figured out where I'm going with this, pay close attention here. We had a son, and a daughter. Yes, it could not be more appropriate that we had one of each gender, so I could do further research for this book. It gives great argument to the environment versus genetic debate. It can sometimes be entertaining to watch the acutely innate differences between the two, in which I must argue for the genetic / gender perspective (it can also drive you crazy sometimes).

My son, Kalvin, exemplifies the literal / linear thinking patterns that tend to dominate males. He is deductive and very logical. I can already see that he will be a handful when he gets older and starts reasoning toward his points. We already call him the "little negotiator," as he clearly identifies things that he wants, and then makes a clear and rational argument for it.

My daughter, Klara, is a different story. I remember when she was still quite young, maybe about a year old, I was competing in a local martial arts tournament. At the end of the tournament, I went up to thank the individual who put on the tournament. She knew I had new addition to the family (Klara), and asked what her demeanor was like. I paused for just a moment, and then replied "calculated." She laughed and said just you wait (that wasn't encouraging). I told my wife later that day that our daughter was inquired about, and I let her know my response. She seemed surprised that I would respond with "calculated." I was surprised that she was surprised. After she thought about it a while, she latched onto my point quite easily.

Our daughter, at the very young age of one, knew exactly how her older brother thought. She seemed to take great joy in taking advantage of this acquired knowledge. It takes a lot to get my daughter upset. That being said, once she is upset, stand back. My son, however, can get upset at absolutely anything. I remember one time we were in Prague visiting my wife's family. I took the kids out for a day so my wife and her mother could spend time together, just the two of them. The kids and I went to town and visited a very old part of the city. They were doing great, and I decided to reward them (and me too) with ice cream. If you didn't know, the portions in Europe tend to be a little smaller than portions here in the States. I ordered us three vanilla ice cream cones (in my horribly misspoken Czech), and then waited for our treat. The first cone I was handed was big enough for all three of us. I was shocked; this certainly wasn't the norm. Since I did not know the Czech word for "stop," I was stuck while we waited for our other two cones.

My original plan was to walk around with the ice creams, but my plans changed with these three gargantuan soft-serve nightmares. We stood outside the ice cream shop where we purchased them and began to eat. My daughter was already a mess. I had put a bib on her, but even she knew that was a joke. She had ice cream all over her face, and she hadn't even taken a bite yet (how the hell does that work?). My son was a little cleaner, but not by much. It was so bad that tourist groups started stopping and taking pictures of them. I'm not kidding. I'm sure someone went back home and talked about the little Czech children eating ice cream at the foot of Charles Bridge in Praha (little did they know, they are only half Czech).

The reason I share this story with you is because about three bites in, my son's ice cream plummeted to the Earth from the cone rim up. This sticks out in my mind so strongly because I was shocked he didn't go into immediate convulsions the moment it happened. He simply gave out a sincere and pitiful "oooaaauuughhh," while he stared down at his lost hopes and dreams of a creamy dessert fulfillment. Before he got an opportunity to rethink his response, I quickly informed him that he could have my ice cream (no way in hell I was going to eat it all anyway), and all was good. I thought this moment would be really terrible, like end of the world terrible, and I was much surprised we had such an easy outcome. The reason this moment is so memorable, is that it is the only time we have had a simple outcome to a "traumatic" experience to date *(see pictures of this at www.womantalkbook.com)*.

My son gets very worked up, and as I said, his sister knows it. She can play well on her own, and oftentimes prefers to. Sometimes, however, she prefers a little drama. When she wants her drama, most of the time she likes it at the expense of her brother. When I say calculated, I want you to understand what I mean. Kalvin has a hard enough time playing on his own. Usually, he wants someone to interact with him. However, on occasion, he will get into his zone and really entertain himself. As parents, his mother and I leave him the hell alone and use that opportunity to do something at least somewhat productive (like take a nap). His sister, however, knows that this is drama time.

Klara will not just go up and mess with him while he is entertaining himself. That wouldn't be near calculated enough. She will wait. I don't just mean regular wait, I mean stealthy wait. I mean peripheral vision wait. I mean strategically wait. I mean calculative wait.

One of the things my son likes to do when he entertains himself is play with his trains. In one particular instance, he was playing for a while with his train, not just with any train, but with his one train that means more to him than breathing. His sister knows this. There he is playing with the train, round the wooden track, over and over again (how anyone could entertain themselves this way is beyond me, I guess you have to be a kid). Lo and behold, a piece of the track managed to work its way loose. My son has learned (through repeated efforts on my part) to repair the track himself. This is usually a two-handed job, so it will require him to put down his train for about 1.7 seconds while this repair takes place. This is when calculation strikes.

During this 1.7 seconds, Klara manages to stop whatever it is she was doing, run all the way across the room, snatch up his favorite train, and sprint away like Carl Lewis before Kalvin even looks up from the track. Calculated! This, of course, sends her brother into a maddening chase at ear-piercing volumes that dogs in the next state can hear. He can't catch her, because if he gets close she runs straight to her mother or her father, and there goes our productivity (napping). Once everything is calmed down and the dust settles, she just waits to do it again.

This tyranny wouldn't be so bad if my son would just figure out that the only reason for this behavior is just to piss him off. What I can't figure out is how he doesn't figure it out, but it is that literal / linear thinking. For example, his favorite train is blue. He has known his colors for a long time, as has his sister. She will take his favorite train and tell him it's red. His brain can't take this; he insists it's blue, to which she replies "no, red." She thinks it's funny as hell. She is able to wrap him around her little finger, to get the results and reactions she desires, all by saying that blue is red. She knows how he thinks, and she comes up with ways to exploit his emotions (and probably psychological well-being) for her own entertainment. I am still trying to figure out at what age girls grow out of doing this to us (if ever).

One time we were vacationing in Florida with the kids. We rented a condo and spent time right at the beach. The kids loved it. However, our daughter was having a hard time coming up with ways to annoy her brother, so she simply created a game called "do you want this," to which he would always reply "yes," to which she would always reply "no, mine!" This would, of course, start a whole series of whining, crying, complaining, and a bunch of other ing's. What would always baffle me is how he couldn't figure out he was being manipulated the whole time.

"What dear? Okay, I'll do it," sorry about that, I'm back now.

Manipulation tends to be second nature to the womenfolk, and it is because of their holistic thinking. The biggest problem is women can easily comprehend how men think, but we men can't begin to comprehend how women think. I mean we get it, we just don't **get** it. What's more important is that we haven't really figured out a way to exploit it (not that we ever would). So the best thing we can do is set up scenarios that help reinforce our own strengths in thinking processes.

This is what I like to call the "Reverse Variable Factor." We men had to come up with something on our own to put the ball in our court. It's not the same as the Variable Factor, and it's not even truly its "reverse." The truth is, it is a very chronological and straight forward set of patterns that just tend to exhaust the female makeup. It's not that they can't figure it out, it's just that they don't care to. It is much simpler to let a man do it (and let him think he knows something they don't).

So what is this reverse variable factor, you ask? I'll give you an example. My wife doesn't know how to turn on the television. I know that sounds absurd, but it's true. Again, it's not that she's not capable, she just isn't interested. She would love to just turn on the TV and have it come on. She tends to get irritated enough having to change the channel, and believe me, she has to do far more than that to watch TV in our house.

Let me preface this with an interesting story about our current television. When we moved into our new home a couple of years ago, we, of course, brought our television with us. It sat on a stand along the wall in our great room. The television happened to be a 65" flat panel LCD (and no, it's not to compensate for a small penis). I thought to myself right away that this would be a great place to hang the television and hide the electronics. That thought sat dormant for about a year until I saw a company advertising tackling this feat for you.

My initial thought was to check with the company and see what they would charge to do this. The more I thought through this process, the more I thought "I could do this myself." The story gets better (as you might have imagined). I drew up a schematic detailing everything I would need to hang the TV and hide all the electronics in a nearby closet. I had electrical requirements figured out, mounting requirements figured out, devices, wiring, RCA's, HDMI's, infrared repeaters, I mean everything. I even found a great deal online for a mounting bracket for thirty bucks that retailed for a hundred and fifty in a local store. As soon as that bracket arrived, I hit the ground running.

Needless to say, my wife wasn't overly thrilled about me tackling this project for a few reasons. For starters, she could really care less whether the TV hung on the wall and the electronics were hidden. She thought it was fine the way it was. Secondly, she knows my personality, and she knew this project would consume me until it was finished. Thirdly, and probably most importantly, she knows Murphy. Yes, Murphy's Law stating that anything that can go wrong will go wrong was certainly not a stranger to us. This project actually wasn't too bad; it just got started wrong.

The problem was I started the project as soon as I opened up the thirty-dollar mounting bracket (so far, so good). I unplugged all the electronics, moved the TV away from the wall, and got everything ready. The reviews on this bracket were great. I remember reading things like "why would anyone pay $ 150 for this thing when you can get it for $30?" They apparently don't have the same TV I have, or their review would have looked much different (if it wasn't removed for language). This bracket didn't even come close to fitting my TV. It was supposed to fit a TV anywhere from 27" to 84". It probably does – for any TV but mine (damn Murphy).

I quickly realized this bracket wasn't going to work, so I zipped over to Best Buy to purchase the $ 150 version. I explained my dilemma, they sympathized, and then happily sold me the one for $ 150, with the assurance this one would work. I got it home, took it apart, and you guessed it, it didn't work. The brackets weren't long enough to stretch across the back of the television where the bolt holes were. So I packed it back up, and headed to Best Buy again. Of course, the gentleman I spoke with before didn't seem to be around (I think he was hiding), but another gentleman was happy to help. I again explained my dilemma, he seemed surprised that the brackets didn't work, but happily sold me a mount that was over $280. "This mounting bracket will work for sure," he told me confidently.

That is where I wish the mounting bracket story ended, but that damn Murphy has to live up to his name. Fortunately the bracket was long enough, but of the 1,000 bolts that came with it, all were too small in diameter to fit in the television (TVs must have gotten thinner and lighter since we bought ours). Now I head to Home Depot (by the way, I'll take monies for plugging retailers if anyone is willing), and I purchase what I think are the necessary bolts. However, I figured I'm going to trump Murphy this time, and also buy some bolts that I don't think are the correct ones. I get them back home and we have success (of course, with the bolts that I thought were correct).

I am now finally ready to "start" this project. I have everything I need. I begin again with the bracket. I put the extenders on to fit the height of the television (success). I get the bolts that I know fit in the back of the television (success). I slide the bolt through the hole in the bracket. Dammit! As you might have guessed, the bolt did not fit through the holes in the bracket in order to make their way to the TV. Long story short on that one, a metal blade and a Sawzall works great on metal brackets.

Now this was just step one of the project, which reconfirmed the reason my wife didn't want me to take it on in the first place (I hate it when she's right). Luck was on my side this time, however, and the rest of the project went pretty smoothly. I'm sure that my wife would like to blame this new ensemble as the reason as to why she can't operate the TV, but it would be a lie as she couldn't operate it even before we hung it on the wall (besides, if you really think about it, what does hanging it change)?

The reason my wife can't operate it is because of the Reverse Variable Factor. See, I can't just have it set to where you can turn on the TV and watch it. I would have no sense of worth if she could do that without me. We have three input devices to choose from when you turn it on, depending on what you want to do. We have the Blu-Ray, the cable box, and the "Czech" DVD player (since U.S. players won't play Czech DVDs, we had to bring one back from Europe. An electrical adapter, scart cable adapter, and a flux capacitor later, we now have one more piece of equipment in my ensemble that contributes to the Reverse Variable Factor). I'm sure my wife will love it when technology advances to the point when your television just "knows" what it is you want to do/watch, but until then, I am in control.

Once the correct input is selected, you must navigate through the appropriate menu. To this day, I don't speak Czech, but I can navigate through the Czech DVD menu better than my native Czech wife can. On top of it, we purchased a sound bar to enhance the sound on that particular television (and when I say "we" I mean "I"), so that adds one more variable to sort through just to begin watching television.

This is actually a simplified version of what we had. I moved all of the stereo/surround equipment to the basement when we (I) hung that television. The basement TV now has Reverse Variable Factor "squared" associated with it. Not only do you have all of the above, but now we have a Wii Game as an additional input, surround sound options, surround sound choices, i.e. music, movie, gaming, etc., and we even have a VCR attached to that system as well (I know, why?). She won't even watch TV in the basement. I honestly don't think she has even turned the television on since this change.

As I said, it's not that they (women) can't figure it out, it's just that they simply don't care to. It's ironic that as holistic processors, women could care less about the sound quality that spills out of the television/stereo system, and us simple/linear men want to be able to hear the individual pebbles hit the ground from the horse gallop of an Indiana Jones movie. We (men) develop these "Reverse Variable Factors" to make us feel like we are in control, like we have one up on them – what would they do without us? We, of course, set up all of these external factors to complement our way of thinking. It is so much "our" way of thinking that my three-year-old son usually turns on the television for his mommy (and flies with ease through all the Reverse Variable Factors that I have strategically set up). We easily understand and remember these "Reverse Variable Factor" processes, and it ensures the women will have no interest in them. In fact, if you are a woman and still reading this, you've already impressed the hell out of me. In case you are a woman and have stopped reading this, I set up this next paragraph to help you out.

IF YOU ARE A WOMAN, START READING AGAIN HERE! Welcome back, we missed you. Yes, the point about the difference between women and technology and men and technology is oftentimes quite evident. I am, of course, generalizing here. There are plenty of women out there who know all about technology, and vice versa for men. Generalizing is much more fun, though (and be *really* honest with yourself about your own strengths and weaknesses as you are reading this). This Reverse Variable Factor does come back to bite us, however, simply because the womenfolk are more well-rounded in their level of thinking.

For example, I for the longest time was asked from my wife how to work different functions on her phone. The key word here is "her" phone. It's not that I "can't" figure it out, it's just that I don't care too....sound familiar? The problem is, I really don't want to go through and figure out all the crap on my own phone, but I spend the time because it is well spent when it comes to the functions I need. My wife, however, just wants a quick path to learn something that more than likely she has no real interest in and will probably never use again. When it came time for us to get new phones, I thought I would be "smart" and suggested that we get the same phone. This way, at least if she asked me about something, I would probably already know or have a good idea. Even if not, I would at least be learning something about my own phone while trying to figure out something on hers.

Just when I think I have it all figured out, that damn Variable Factor pops up again. This was clearly an advantage to have the same phones. Additional advantages for getting the same phones:

1. They are the same, so they can have similar carrying cases
2. They have the same power cord, so one is readily available
3. We are "even Steven" on the technology / upgrade side
4. We can easily share things
5. We can knowingly work each other's phone

I did find a few disadvantages to having the same phone, which is why I damned the Variable Factor at the beginning of this paragraph. I will give you the disadvantages as they directly correlate to the advantages listed above…

1. Quit taking my phone to work and leaving me to discover I am stuck trying to do business all day on your phone
2. Where the hell is my power cord
3. I know you want a better phone than me
4. I don't care
5. Please leave my phone the hell alone

So, as smart as I thought I was being at suggesting we get the same phone, I really gained nothing in the end. Such is life. You would think I'd have learned it by now, that there is no "one upping" them. They have thought things through to the nth degree, and we can't compete.

Women simply think differently than men. Need more proof? There are some words you can say, and men and women interpret them entirely differently. If you don't know what I mean, here is a list of examples a friend of mine shared with me that will help you better understand.

1. VULNERABLE
    a. Woman: Fully opening up one's self emotionally to another
    b. Man: Playing football without a cup
2. COMMUNICATION
    a. Woman: The open sharing of thoughts and feelings with one's partner
    b. Man: Leaving a note before taking off on a fishing trip with the boys
3. COMMITMENT
    a. Woman: A desire to get married and raise a family
    b. Man: Trying not to hit on other women while out with this one
4. ENTERTAINMENT
    a. Woman: A good movie, concert, play or book
    b. Man: Anything that can be done while drinking beer
5. FLATULENCE
    a. Woman: An embarrassing byproduct of indigestion
    b. Man: A source of entertainment, self-expression, male bonding
6. MAKING LOVE
    a. Woman: The greatest expression of intimacy a couple can achieve
    b. Man: Call it whatever you want just as long as we do it
7. REMOTE CONTROL
    a. Woman: A device for changing from one TV channel to another
    b. Man: A device for scanning through all 375 channels every 5 minutes
8. THINGY
    a. Woman: Any part under a car's hood
    b. Man: The strap fastener on a woman's bra*

Get the idea about what I mean by "thinking differently"? If it ain't broke, fix it. That's been my motto ever since that one day in my kitchen I so "cleverly" educated my wife on the sayings of the American people. Whether it be America, the Czech Republic, Iceland, it doesn't matter. Men and women don't always speak the same language. When I say "how does this thingy come undone," she goes out to look at the car. Speaking of cars, there are only a few types of cars if you ask my wife. There a red ones, black ones, green ones, blue ones, (you get the idea). Which brings me to the next chapter on driving, and fasten your seatbelts for this one......

(* These were jokes that were shared with me by a friend over the internet. An attempt was made to find the original author, but proved to be unsuccessful. Author unknown).

Chapter 7
Driving

    I imagine you think this is the chapter where I'm going to let the women have it? You would be correct! Just kidding. Actually, I think it is the perfect time to reiterate the concept of the Reverse Variable Factor. I feel the automotive industry is typically dominated by men (I "feel" this way because I have no statistical data to back that up). This being said, it shouldn't be too surprising that women revert back to the "I don't care" mentality. As I mentioned in the last chapter, my wife typically only differentiates cars by their color. While she probably falls to one side of the bell curve here with that analogy, I don't think it's too far off the norm. If men typically dominate the automotive industry, then cars are typically built with the concept of other men in mind (which means powerful and loud if you're old school). Somewhere along the line, someone's wife talked them into designing and putting in a vanity mirror.

    My wife didn't get her first car until she was 27 years old. She was from the big city of Prague, the capital of the Czech Republic, with massive public transportation, and really had no need for a car. Truth be told, I would probably not own a car if I lived in Prague either. However, I grew up in the capital of Kansas, so I've been driving since I was 14 years old. I couldn't wait to get behind the wheel and all that it represented. I took driving classes, but that was a piece of cake after my father had already taught me how to drive. My father was definitely old school when it came to learning how to drive. When I was a kid, we had a 1960 Ford pickup truck we nicknamed "the tank." Dad drove this to work every day. I remember you could see the street through the floorboards, and if I had to give it a color I would call it "prime" green.

    This truck was my father's "favorite old chair" if that paints an appropriate analogy. Part of me felt honored he would choose this vehicle for me to learn to drive on. The other 99 percent of me was pissed off and horrified. When I was 14, I probably weighed 115 pounds soaking wet. When they made this 1960 Ford pickup truck, I don't think the word "power" had even been invented yet, let alone the thought of putting it in steering, brakes, or windows. To turn that behemoth of a monster on my part required a pulled muscle(s) and a prayer, but my father's logic was "if you can learn to drive this, then you can drive anything." This truck had a granny gear and an automatic chock. It took a special séance just to get the damn thing started. However, I learned on that, and now I can drive anything. (Ironically enough every automobile I've owned since then has been a step up and I've never truly needed the "you can drive anything" skill set. Maybe that was his plan?)

At 15, I finally upgraded to driving the 1980 Toyota Corolla. This was great. It was more my size, and I thought I could actually "drive" this car. My father, however, wasn't willing to accept this on blind faith. So the first time I got to take it out, my father went with me with a glass of water and set it on the dash. I'm not making this up, that's my dad. I wasn't going to get to drive this car unless I could perform his driving feats without spilling a drop. The planets must have been aligned that day because somehow I passed (and have never driven that way since).

This was my driving training, and now let me give you my vast experience in mechanics. When I was 16, I got a job and bought my first car. I'll date myself just a little bit here first by saying the car was a 1976 Volkswagen Rabbit, and secondly by saying I paid $ 650 for it. I was out at Toys R Us one day with my daughter and noticed that one of the children's drive-around "toy" cars cost, ironically enough, $ 650. That dated me hard (reminds me of how my father talked about how a can, excuse me, bottle of Pepsi cost a nickel). Anyway, the Germans sure got their money's worth out of me on "parts" for that Rabbit. If you can think of it, I probably had to work on it or replace it.

This was irritating as hell when I was 16, but probably good for me in the long run to get the experience I did repairing that car. It amazed me the amount of stuff my father knew about cars, and he tried to teach me what he could on my '76 P.O.S. A few of the things he taught me even stuck (mind you, not many). That being said, I was at least exposed to a certain level of mechanics. Although my wife is a great driver despite her lesser experience (I, of course, better say this in case she actually reads this book), her experience in mechanics….not quite so much. I will humor you with our first "real" scuffle since we got married, and I'll pray she doesn't kill me for sharing it with you.

One morning we traveled to Kansas City to visit with the INS office (procedure, of course). For some reason, we took my father's car on the trip. I really don't remember why, but irrelevant for this story except for the fact it wasn't my car and I wasn't super familiar with it. Even that is irrelevant as I lead into the fact that I had left the headlights on while we were in the INS meeting. The meeting wasn't short, and by the time that we got back out to the car, there was no way that battery was going to get the car started.

At this point I was fairly frustrated. Frustrated with the INS for all the formalities we had to go through, frustrated with myself for leaving the headlights on, and frustrated that I was going to have to locate someone with jumper cables to get this car going again. My wife asked why I was so frustrated, so I informed her we were going to need to find someone with some jumper cables. She didn't understand my irritation; "Just ask someone," she said. That is all well and good if you're a woman. Any man who has jumper cables will be willing to help out a woman in distress. Any man who asks is incredibly annoying and will promptly be told that "sorry, I don't have any jumper cables." (You may remember a similar scenario when men vs. women ask for directions in Chapter 1 of this book, "In The Beginning…)

Long story short, she decided to test my theory and ask for help herself (which she promptly got from the first gentleman she asked). Here is where the story gets interesting. I was already frustrated and wasn't thinking through my wife's "automotive / mechanics" experience. She shortly walks up to me and hands me a pair of jumper cables. That's it. Needless to say, my frustration has now increased even more. I look around, and I see a gentleman staring at us from across the parking lot, standing next to his car, with what I swear was a visible question mark hovering over his head. I quickly gave him the "come on over here" wave, and he nodded his head as a sign of relief (I'm sure he was high with anticipation as to what was going to occur next).

My response to my wife was something like "we'll probably need another car to connect these to," in possibly not the most pleasing tone. As we got the car started and drove off in a bit of a tiff with each other, I can only imagine the INS officers sitting inside watching, and then stamping our file "approved" saying "Yeah, these two are definitely in a real marriage." Fortunately, enough time has passed that I can joke about it (I hope), and in my wife's defense, how the hell was she supposed to know that you needed another car to "jump" from. I remember when I was a teenager, one of the male employees at my first job told a female employee she was running low on blinker fluid on her car. She asked about it on her next oil change, and that is how she found out there was no such thing. This same person also told her she needed to let the old air out of her tires and put new air in (and she did it).

I only mention these instances to verify my point that us men have set up a typical "Reverse Variable Factor" in much of the automotive area. Again, it's not that women can't figure things out, but they just don't care. Men get very preoccupied with our cars. Some even give their cars girl's names (I'm sure some Freudian psychologist would have a field day with that one). The point is that we all have our areas of interest and expertise, and to spend any energy into an area of "non" interest would seemingly be a tremendous waste of time. I know that I try to muster up every facial expression of interest every time my wife asks me to look at just about anything in a magazine or online. I just don't really care to look at it, think about it, match it, build it, or buy it. It's just not me, but I care that she cares and that's why I keep looking.

All of this is okay. We are in such a highly sensitized society now that it's hard to categorize wants, needs, and desires by gender. As I mentioned before, my wife is a fine driver. However, if we are all out as a family, I typically do the driving. I'm a man, I want to drive, I need to drive, and I desire to drive. It is just incredibly difficult for me to sit there with her driving (it does happen on occasion). I'm often reminded of something a college professor stated. He taught Political Science and Political Corruption. One day, and I can't remember the original topic, but he spoke about the "stereotypes" of men and women. He argued they each had their role in a marriage. This got some of the class stirring, but he quieted them down when he asked, "Who does the driving when the whole family is together, and who writes out the Christmas cards?" That summed it up for most of us.

As I've said, it's okay. We should embrace these differences, stand up for what we believe and are interested in, and not be so sensitive about it. For example, I'm interested in the study of limitations in vision. I throw myself into this study every time it rains when I'm driving and decide what speed to set the wipers on (if at all). My father is interested in brakes, so he tests them to the limits *every single time* he makes a *stop* while driving (the imaginary one on my side of the car sure as hell doesn't work). Ironically enough, he's also interested in fuel combustion, so he tests this to the limit every time he *starts* while driving. However, he isn't alone, and I would imagine most of his company would be other men. This doesn't shock any of us, and it's certainly not going to change. In fact, I think it gets worse the older you get until you finally hit that "where's the beef" stage and can't drive at all (there, I just dated myself again).

I have a solution though. You see, the government is too big and too limited by its size to give you the real deal on a driving exam. The DMV has a booklet to study the rules of driving, but they are pretty much worthless. How do I know? Look at all the drivers on the road who shouldn't be there. I took the privilege of going through some of Kansas' driving rules. I can only assume (ass u me) that they are relatively the same for most states. Let's take a look at them, and see how they stack up to the male and female driver.

1. ***"Drive in the right-hand lane:** The left land is for passing or turning."* Okay, I don't have a "male" and "female" comparison for this one. I only have an "idiot" and "non-idiot" comparison. This seems like a no-brainer to me, and I feel like reaching out and choking someone if I have to move to the right lane to pass somebody. There doesn't seem to be any rhyme or reason as to the demographics of this type of driver either. They tend to be young, old, male, female, black, white, which is why I have generally classified them as "idiot" and "non-idiot." So if you ever have to deal with this (and I know you do), just pleasantly supply them with your driving finger, which I am now calling the idiot finger.
2. ***"Drive in Proper Lane:** Never move from one lane to another until you make certain that you can do so safely. This means watching for safe clearance to the side, ahead and behind your vehicle. Do not rely solely on your mirror when checking for clearance. Look over your*

shoulder to check the 'blind spot' your mirror does not cover. You must signal your intentions to other drivers by using turn signals. But remember, a signal does not grant you the right to change lanes. You must wait until it is safe to do so. Remember: A bicycle or motorcycle in a traffic lane is entitled to the full use of that lane. Do not drive in a manner that will deprive the cyclist of full use of his lane." Okay, first of all if you are a 3,000-pound car and I am a simple cyclist, you better believe you're going to deprive me of that lane if you start to move into it. As a matter of fact, I will gladly get the hell out of the way and give you all of the room you want (I am going to curse at you and call you an idiot, but I'll move). So again, I think this isn't specific to a gender, but I think we can look at a "reason" for a lack of driving in proper lanes from a gender specific point of view. If you are a woman and you have failed to drive in your proper lane, it is probably because of one of the following reasons.

- *a.* You are either looking for something or have found something
- *b.* You have to LOL, BFF, TTYL or TTFN on your phone because it is oh so urgent (that last one is a Winnie the Pooh/Tigger reference if you didn't catch it)
- *c.* That lipstick is not going to put itself on
- *d.* You are a woman, and you deserve both/all lanes

If you are a man, you may have some reasons too…

- *a.* You just don't give a damn
- *b.* Idiot

I know there are plenty more reasons for both women and men to not drive in the proper lane, but I think we've covered the most important ones.

3. **"Stay out of another driver's blind spot:** *The blind spots are on both sides of the car. Traveling in a position*

where the driver ahead of you cannot observe your vehicle in the rearview mirror is a dangerous practice- the driver might pull out in front of you to pass a car. Either stay behind or go around." We can put this one another way – if you would like to be hit, drive in the blind spot. This is an area that if you camp out in it, you're just asking for it. For women, I think it may be that you are just unaware there are other drivers on the road. For men, I think you are slowly trying to creep to the car next to you just to see if there is a hot woman driving it. Either way, stay safe! Stay out of this blind spot area. The DMV would be wise to call this section either "hello, there are other people on the road" or "she's probably ugly." Think of all of the car insurance claims we wouldn't have to file.

4. **"Maintain Safe Distance:** *Another good method is to watch the car ahead of you. When it passes some reference point, such as a telephone pole, then count "one-thousand-one, one-thousand-two". If you pass the same spot before you are through counting, you are following too closely. When you are following vehicles which often stop (buses, post office vans) you should allow more following distance than usual. When driving in bad weather, you should increase following distance 3 or 4 seconds."* Okay, so here is a slam on men. I don't know what it is, but most men seem to follow other cars too closely. Yes, this can be dangerous, particularly with the response time of a lot of drivers I've seen on the road. I think it is our pressing attitudes of wanting to always go faster. And let's face it, there are times when it's appropriate. If you're a man and are ever stopped for this reason, politely explain to the officer that it's not your fault, that it's simply genetics. Explain that procreation is simply hardwired into your genes, and that you couldn't help but try to mount the car in front of you. Just please make sure you have at least one good friend with savings.

5. **"Backing Up:** *Before backing your vehicle it is a good practice to walk completely around the vehicle to be sure no person or obstacle is behind you."* Before we continue

with the rest of the state's guide, let me point out that if there is someone crouching behind your car who isn't visible from any vantage point even from the front of the car, then you have my permission to just run that idiot over. They would more than likely be there to cause you harm anyway, so bonus points. Okay continuing..."*Before backing you should look to the front, sides and rear, and continue to look to the rear while backing. Do not depend on your mirror. Backing slowly into the proper traffic lane with a minimum of movement. Follow the same rules when backing into traffic lanes after being parked at an angle. Except for backing into a parking space, it is never advisable to back up on a public street or road. If you back out of a driveway, always back into the nearest lane and proceed from there. NEVER back across other traffic lanes.*" I don't know what it is, but in my personal experience men and women tend to view backing up very differently. Men seem to love it and women seem to hate it. I don't know why it is, maybe men have messed up too many times and would love to "back up" and try things over again. Maybe it's because women like it better frontwards (interpret that one however you want). Either way, we could probably sum it up by saying women should probably get more practice at it, and men should slow down when they do it.

These are just a few things the DMV has that could be improved upon, but I think we can take it one step further here. Regardless of gender, a few things have been "omitted" from state driving manuals, and I think we should address them. If you find yourself with time on your hands, by all means try to get them added in your area. I would, but I have been officially banned from the DMV except for when law requires license renewal.

First of all, I think it's important to address the functions of some of the equipment in the car. I mean, seatbelts and mirrors are addressed, but what about other items? For instance, maybe we shouldn't assume everyone knows the vertical pedal on the right makes the car go? I only say this because I run into people all the time (not literally but close) who don't seem to know the function of this pedal. This lack of knowledge alone is enough to incite road rage in any one of the 56 cars following this person. However, I would like to offer a suggestion that will reduce road rage as well as risk of heart attack or brain aneurysms. Simply pass them. I know it sounds crazy and simple, but I've started to do this and I've loved the benefit. I move into the lane of oncoming traffic (if none is coming) or into a center turning lane and drive around them. No need to be angry, no need to do it aggressively, just simply do it. The only drawback to this solution is if a police officer sees you, but I am convinced that if you explain your situation and reasons, he/she will empathize and let you off the hook. All of it could be solved anyway if the DMV would just print in their book that to make the car go, it is the "vertical pedal on the right."

Speaking of speed, there should be a section about speed limits clearly indicating they are not "suggestions." I say this because we all know we can be ticketed for driving in excess of the speed limit. This is understandable; the name says it all, it is the "limit" of the speed. However, I think one should be ticketed if he/she is driving under the speed limit. I'll give you turning, but outside of that, let's go, people.

"Immediate lane" should be better defined in the DMV manual, as well. I think a lot of people, men and women alike, think "immediate" lane means the first lane they feel like pulling into as opposed to the closest lane to them. The DMV could fix this by simply having a terminology section that defines "immediate lane" as: The lane that is first, nearest, closest – idiot.

I believe there should also be something written about society's social role in certain situations when it comes to driving. For example, if someone drives for more than sixteen blocks with their blinker on, you should shoot them and put them out of their misery. If you don't understand that the little blinking arrow on your dash is correlated to the lights on the outside of your car, then accept the repercussions.

Speaking of lights, maybe it should also be formally stated that when those red lights light up in the back of the car, this means that the person in front of you is slowing down or stopping. Either way, it is a reasonable, safe assumption that you should alter your speed. My suggestion is to slowly depress your own brake pedal, and as best as possible match your speed to the new speed of the vehicle in front of you that displayed those pretty red lights. I like this approach better than the "keep your own speed right up until there is sixteen inches between you and the vehicle in front of you, then aggressively and angrily slam on your brakes as hard as you can while making your eyes big enough to be seen better than anything in the rear view mirror of the vehicle on front of you." You know who you are.

One final suggestion is about when a lane is ending that you're in. It may be a simple merge situation, or it may be due to road construction, but there are times when lanes end. A reasonable driver (again, man or woman) will identify that the lane is ending by one of the fifteen signs indicating so long before it actually ends. Oftentimes, these signs will even indicate a number of feet in which this particular lane will end. So why IN THE WORLD someone would wait until the VERY LAST SECOND to try to escape the lane they are in that is now gone is beyond me. You better believe I'm not going to let you in, and I simply don't understand how you would be surprised by that fact.

Truth be told, everybody knows how to drive correctly. If you don't believe me, then pay attention the next time you are driving when there's a police officer around. I can ALWAYS know there is a cop around literally by the way I see people drive. Everyone knows what the vertical pedal on the right is, everyone knows what an immediate lane is, and everyone knows what a brake light is. This, of course, only infuriates me more because people *could* be driving like this all the time. It's okay, though, I've learned to live longer by simply driving around.

All things considered I think it would be helpful to add these relevant items on the DMV test. At least people couldn't say "I didn't know."

Chapter 8
Educational Reading

Here is my challenge to each of you as readers. Many topics have not been covered in this book that would be helpful to each gender. I challenge you to come up with your own material and information to share with other readers. We need more books to educate the sexes. I will share with you here some relevant topics that would be helpful. This is in no way a complete list, but it is a start. Someone please tackle these topics and get the information out there to those that need it.

Topics of education for women to cover:

Estrogen:

Both men and women contain levels of estrogen within their bodies. There are, of course, typically higher amounts of estrogen in women. We should both love and hate these higher amounts of estrogen. We should love it because estrogen helps give women their womanly figures that we men tend to appreciate so much. We should hate it because higher amounts of estrogen bring on a swarm of other emotional riptides that we men have a hard time understanding.

My wife told me a story a co-worker shared. This co-worker spoke of how his 14-year-old daughter started down the stairs one morning. This father simply shared with her, "You look really nice today." Upon receiving the compliment, his daughter shouted at her father, "How could you say something like that to me?" then stormed back upstairs. Estrogen is the only explanation for this situation.

If you're like me, then upon hearing this story you developed a slight to medium headache. There is no quickly figuring out what went wrong in this situation. It is chaos theory at its finest. Somewhere in the world a butterfly flapped its wings, which provoked this malicious attack on this now stupefied father who only tried to give his daughter a compliment.

One of the funniest examples of the effects of increased estrogen levels comes from a movie. In "The Longest Yard," starring Adam Sandler, a prison guard has his steroid pills replaced with estrogen pills. Here we have an example of both ends of the spectrum. We have a butch, steroid-infused prison guard, who is reduced to a sniffling little crybaby due to these changes. The change is, of course, exaggerated for the sake of humor, but definitely hit the nail on the head in the laugh department. What was most funny was watching the other guards try to understand and relate to the changes that were taking place in the estrogen-infused guard right before them. You could quickly see that they would rather deal with the thieving and murderous behavior of the inmates, for it was easier to deal with.

So please, somebody out there. Gather all that you will need to help explain the true and measureable effects of estrogen. In particular, write it for men to better understand when it is and isn't appropriate to give compliments. I am anticipating that all things considered, this will be about an 8,500-page book.

Emotions:

It isn't a huge leap to transition from estrogen to emotions. In fact, I'm sure that at least 3,000 of the 8,500 pages in the estrogen book will cover emotions directly. That being said, I think it is relevant to have a book that only covers emotions.

The most obvious topic of choice when talking about emotions is how to deal with them. Emotions aren't a bad thing. In fact, they are a tremendous and powerful asset. Emotions are what we use to drive to fruition our most wanted desires. They are the backbone of accomplishment and achievement. They are truly an energetic force to be reckoned with. The previous are examples of how emotions can benefit us if we channel them effectively. But what about if we don't channel them effectively? Let's look at a conversation between a couple who is trying to make dinner plans. In this scenario, let's put the woman at a high emotional state (you can insert whatever reason you want).

Man: "So where would you like to go for dinner tonight?"

Woman: "Oh, I don't care, you decide."

Man: "How about that new restaurant that opened up nearby?"

Woman: "I'm not really in the mood for steak; how about someplace else?"

Man: "There is the Mexican place downtown?"

Woman: "You know Mexican food makes me sleepy, I thought you wanted to go do something after dinner?"

Man: "So…..where would you like to go for dinner tonight?"

Woman: "I told you I don't care, you decide! Why do I always have to decide everything? Why don't you take charge for once in your life? It's not like this decision will be the bane of our existence! Just pick a place and let's go eat so we can still have some time left to do something this evening. I'm going to be ready in 5 minutes (really 45) so just pick a place already, and we'll go there. While I finish getting ready, you have a place in mind. Then we will get in the car, and you can drive there and surprise me. It is really not that difficult."

Man: "????????"

So while the woman is getting ready, the man thinks about where to go. He can see that there is a certain charge of emotion in the air. He is not sure what it is about, but he realizes that this dinner decision could indeed actually be the bane of his existence. He knows that steak is out and he knows that Mexican is out, but he still has several options left. During his 5-minute (45minute / approaching an hour) evaluation process, he decides on a restaurant nearby. He figures it is close, it has a variety of items on the menu, and it is moderately priced. So, he can't be in trouble for it taking too long, he can't be in trouble for going someplace with too specific of a cuisine, and he can't be in trouble for blowing the budget. Jackpot!

> Woman: (one hour and ten minutes later): "Okay, I'm ready, let's go."

They get in the car and drive to the nearby restaurant. He is watching her expression, which looked a little sour when they left, and has seemed thus far to remain unchanged. They walk into the restaurant, sit down, and look over the menu. The waiter comes over and asks the lady what she would like first. She, of course, is still deciding so she asks him to start with his order. He orders something off the menu, which takes 4.5 seconds, and she now knows what she wants. She orders something off the menu with four substitutions and adjustments. They wait in uncomfortable silence for the meal to arrive. The conversation continues to be minimal for reasons that he still does not quite comprehend. So to break the silence, he decides to go out on a limb.....

> Man: "So.....how is your food?"

> Woman: "We should have gone somewhere for steak."

It may never be known by this man what the original emotional charge was about. He will spend some time thinking about it. He will wonder if he did something, or if the outburst was related to something else. Most importantly, he will wonder if there was a way he could have identified this storm ahead of time and taken appropriate shelter.
    So if anyone has any the time, energy, and effort, please research this matter and give some insight to us men. If we have a better handle on how emotions work, I'm sure we can be perceptive enough to help, or at least get out of the way. I have developed a

theory that there is a small chance these emotional times are used simply for control. I'm not saying all the time, but there are times when it does occur. Take my daughter. There are times when she can absolutely lose it because of, oh I don't know, anything.

Say, for example, her brother gets to watch his show on TV, and not hers. She will go right into hysteria. She will open up the floodgates and let the waterworks go and everything. This, in and of itself, shouldn't seem too alarming or distressing. After all, she is upset about not getting to watch a show of her choosing; she is emotional. The disturbing part comes in when she lets out a happy and joyful "YEAH!" on the turn of a dime when you tell her that she can pick a new show in 10 minutes. That simply has to be a tool of manipulation and control. I'm sure this technique only gets better with time and age.

So here are some situations that some writer out there (more than likely a woman) could give us fellas some heads up on. If we could identify the emotional brewing early enough, then we wouldn't have to hear these comments.

- I don't know where you WANT me to put your golf clubs, but I can tell you where they are GOING to go if you don't get them out of my way.
- After all these years, I thought you would know what I would order by now, you selfish, unobservant, insensitive bastard.
- I'm thinking about trying kickboxing.
- If Julie is so damn interesting, then why don't you go sleep over at her and Tom's house tonight?
- Not tonight, I have a headache.
- Not tomorrow night, I will have a headache then too.
- How about I just let you know when my headache goes away?
- (Crying uncontrollably) I just don't know why she doesn't (sniffles and sobs), and why I can't (more sniffles and sobs some more), you know what I mean?
- If I was going to kill you, how do you think I would do it?
- Go ahead, see what happens...

These are just some of the countless scenarios we men wish we had some foresight about. If we could identify the red flags that lead up to these comments, then maybe we could do something differently to potentially ward off these "unpleasantries." We are willing, but someone needs to meet us halfway. So please, if you have the knowledge and the drive, put a book out there on emotions and how to deal with them. I will be the first to buy it.

Money and what it's for:

When I was preparing this section of this chapter, I got brave and asked my wife for some input. She summed up all that I was originally thinking with one simple statement, "I just like to spend it – and by that I mean not on anything useful." This is what I always thought, but I didn't want to be the one to say it.

So now that the statement has been made, we will now go into some of the specifics of what these things are. Before we do so, let's address a couple of universal principles that precede the specifics. The first universal principle is to know that no matter what item it is that you are looking for, there is another item out there that is just a *little bit* better. This is probably the main reason for the second universal principle, which is that there are always items that need to be returned. Oftentimes, women buy items they know they are going to return. As a man, I see a much simpler process, which is to not buy the item in the first place. That's just me, though, and we can discuss that more in the section on what men think money is for.

Clothes are one of the items that usually come home with the intention of going right back to the store. One apparent reason is the use of trick mirrors and trick lighting inside the stores. If we are following the concepts contained within this book, we'll notice an incorporation of the pattern here. A woman will be browsing in the store. Suddenly, she will see a shirt she can't live without. God Himself/Herself put that shirt there for her to buy. To deny buying this shirt would be the same as denying God. Not only that, the shirt is normally $899.99, (rounded to $1,000 when she tells her husband), on sale today only for $19.99 (rounded to $15 when she tells her husband). She asks him if he has any money on him so she can make this purchase, and he, of course, has to give her $40. This process in and of itself, while exhausting to the typical man, is still tolerable. The breaking point for us is when, after all of that, she takes the shirt back (and then gives him back $10 because $15 has now been "re-rounded").

Yes, this is one of the many joys of money for women. Another joy women spend money on is hair. It will be argued this money is spent for their men. Don't be fooled by this. Two points could be made about men and how they feel about hair expenses. The first point is that they'll probably not notice after the hair is done (and oftentimes even if it is drastic), and second, since they don't usually notice, then why spend the money. I personally go get my hair cut when it gets long, and I get it cut the same every time. My needs, however, are rather simple. At this point, I'm just glad I have hair to cut. Women tend to strive for higher ambitions.

The real reason women get their hair "done" on a regular basis tends to be two-fold. First, they do it to get the attention, not from their men (or other men for that matter), but rather from other women. They do this because they get the attention, love, and affection women will give them since the men won't. Somehow, this helps women with their self-esteem pertaining to men. Go figure. Secondly, women tend to form special bonds with their hair stylists. Whoever is there cutting hair that day, is who I have cut my hair. Women schedule their hair appointments way in advance, and they always request the same person. This bond that is formed tends to be stronger than blood brothers. How I would love to be a fly on the wall during one of these hair appointments. I am sure these are times when the Woman Talk Code is readjusted as needed. It is probably something like high court. The "gavel comb" is dropped and the meeting commences.

"Here ye, here ye, here ye. May this meeting come to order for this session update on Woman Talk Code. In Section 412, subset 3,642, the word *man* needs to be changed in this instance to *conniving little weasel* and will remain that way until further notice."

In the distance we hear a hair dryer go from "low" to "high" while someone's hair is violently teased. "All in favor, please indicate so." All of a sudden flat irons clap in supportive unison. "Let it also be known, if you see Deborah's husband out in public you are to tell him that his new tattoo looks stupid, and he's lucky Deborah did not leave him. Also, if Mark doesn't notice what I am doing to Susie's hair here today, and compliment her on it, then no one is to speak to him again, EVER!" This goes on for about an hour, with multiple adjustments to *the Code* and instructions on how to carry them out. After the normal amount of allotted time for having your hair done, they decide to wrap it up. The "gavel comb" is struck on the on the hair-littered work station. The smell of hot rollers and hair coloring suddenly becomes more prominent now that "business" is over. Relevant adjustments are made to *the Code* and men remain oblivious. The only thing that seems different is that Mark cannot figure out why no one will speak to him?

This is clearly money well spent for the ladies. They get to change their hair, complain about their men, adjust the Code, and have leverage to be angry with us men if they want to. Makes sense to me. It seems a lot of money women spend are on things to "change" their appearance. Hair, nails, clothes, shoes, makeup, just to name a few. I still haven't figured out what all of this is for, outside of the obvious of being able to put us men in trouble if we don't notice.

Women, of course, like to spend money on many other things men simply don't understand. I've only mentioned a few here, but more are out there. Maybe if someone took it upon themselves to write about it, and educate the male population, we could be enlightened. Like why do women buy things that have a smell that infiltrates the male nose to the point of not being able to complete a thought? We should know why. Someone help us out.

Time and what it's for:

Time is one thing in the universe that is a great equalizer. No matter who you are, what you do, time is the same for all of us. It doesn't care if you are rich or broke, black or white, male or female – you can't get around time. Men and women tend to view time a little differently. As this concept of time is universal, and because we are transitioning into topics for men to cover very shortly, we will address time and what it's for from both the female and male perspectives right here and now.

Although time is equal for everyone, many men foolishly think they can somehow get more of it. We do this in many ways, including the need to try and make everything faster so we can save time. We might make the lawnmower faster, we might drive faster, we might try to clean up faster, all with the intention of "saving time." I've put in an extensive study to measure the quality of output to find an "attempt to save time" to "actually saving time" correlation.

To initiate this study, I first tried to get a sampling of 100 men to create a baseline. However, 98 of them were "too busy" trying to save time, so I was left with a sampling of 2. With the use of these two men, I initiated statistical analysis using algebra, calculus, geometry, trial and error, double-blind studies, and a little bit of addition to figure out a mathematical formula measuring the amount of time spent trying to "save time" (X), to actual "time saved" (Y). What I was hoping to find was that men figured something out, and that we might have a formula that looks something like this…

$$X=2Y$$

As I delved further in the study and my optimism started to shrink, I was hoping to at least find some results that looked something like this….

$$X=Y$$

Unfortunately, my study actually revealed results that looked closer to this…

$$2X=Y$$

These results were a little disconcerting, but no matter how I worked the math it kept coming out the same. What scared me was how similar this was to another mathematical equation that proved itself earlier in my studies. That formula looked like this...

$$1 \geq 2$$

At first this mathematical realization scared me, but then I remembered the concept of yin and yang and knew there is always an "equal but opposite" out there in the universe. What I had truly discovered was the opposite version of "female mathematics." When we have a concept like $1 \geq 2$, we have measure of input that actually bears an output result that is at least doubled in nature. When trying to save time, we have a measure of input that actually bears an output result of at minimum ½ in nature.

This discovery was indeed alarming, but you can't argue the math. Plus you can't argue with my large sampling of 2 either. That may seem like a small sampling, but the fact that 98% of the rest of the attempted sampling were "too busy" to even participate further reinforces my results. To keep the language simple, we will always refer to this "halving of the output" as "male mathematics."

To be honest, despite all of the male attempts to save time, I think women may actually have an upper hand in this area. I am, of course, talking about the ability to multitask. This ability allows women to do two, sometimes three or four things, at once. I have always been envious of this ability. As we discussed before, man's linear thinking patterns simply don't allow us to operate this way. I'm glad we don't have to breathe in and out at the same time, otherwise mankind may have gone extinct a long time ago.

Women, please do not say anything important to a man when he is reading, watching TV (or looking at any kind of screen for that matter), combing his hair, brushing his teeth, thinking, or performing any other remedial task. We are already occupied and otherwise engaged. If you want to say something important to a man, it is a good idea to start by sitting him down in a quiet room and making sure he is looking directly at you. At this point, you'll want to inform him you are not seducing him, so that way he can stop thinking about sex and his possibility of having it – as this will be his default thought process. Then you will want to speak slowly, repeat yourself, and have him repeat what you said back to you. Only then will you know with 100% accuracy that he heard and understood you (it may not be a bad idea to ask him to stop breathing in and out while he is listening, too, just remind him to start back up again).

On the flip side, men should always be cautiously aware of what we say and do when women are around. Women are very perceptive beings and can absorb many things at once. A woman could be watching TV, changing a baby, and going through some mail and still see you trying to sneak off and go (insert favorite activity that you used to do all the time before you were in a loving, sincere, beneficial committed relationship).

That being said, man's attempt to save time appears to form out of envy for women's ability to multitask. Ironically, the harder man tries at replicating this skill, the less "time" he ends up with. The less "time" he ends up with, the fewer very important samplings they are able to participate in to greatly benefit aspiring authors.

Another universal resource about time is both men and women wishing they could go "back in it." The attempt to right the wrongs and all the implications this would bring is flattering to anyone. This, of course, cannot be done, as it would be the end of time as we know it. There would be so many parallel time universes out there of people trying to fix things in their lives that there would no longer be a universal "time." Probably the best thing both men and women can do to replicate going back in time is to look at their pasts and do something different in the present if they desire a different future. Both sexes, wrap your mind around that one.

So what do men and women prefer to do with their time? If they are in a happy relationship, then couples will work on spending more time together. If they are in an unhappy relationship, they will work on spending more time apart. Time with the kids, time in the sun, time reading (this one is very important).

Men will work in time with other men. This is done so they can spend their time doing one thing and not be expected to comprehend anything else going on. Sometimes men will get very ambitious and work at watching the game AND drinking beer (this takes much focus and concentration). Men will spend their time taking things apart, finding out which t-shirt best matches their jeans, and believe it or not, figuring out a way to hear what their significant other is saying while at the same time doing something else – just not very successfully.

Women will work in time with other women. This is done so they can be listened to and understood while also breathing in and out. They will spend a lot of time brushing up on the latest styles and trends so they will always know what to (and what not to) wear. Women spend time on their hair and their nails (and multitask by updating the Woman Talk code as we discussed previously), and they most fervently spend their time coming up with excuses to not have sex.

The reality of the situation is that, although time is equal for all, women do tend to have the upper hand in this department. The ability to multitask is very admirable, and something most men will never understand. Balancing time and spending it wisely is probably the best any of us can do. I am glad you have chosen wisely by spending your time reading this book. It is now a good idea to spend some time writing about time and what it is for. If you are a man, focus on this task and nothing else or it will never get done. If you are a women, go ahead and write about it while you are juggling if you want. Either way, let's get it out there so that we can all benefit.

Topics of education for men to cover:

Testosterone:

What about this magnificent hormone? Channeled properly, it can be used to build bridges, skyscrapers, and cities. However, most of the time it is just responsible for fast driving and bar fights. Like anything else, testosterone is best when properly balanced. Too much can make you act like a steroid-infused idiot, bench pressing cars and yelling at the iron for being hot. Too little can make you disconnected and apathetic. Most people, however, have an appropriate balance and are able to function in day-to-day life.

While both men and women produce testosterone, it is typically produced in higher amounts in men. Women should be thankful. This is what typically gives men their large muscles, and rock-hard bodies women like. Men, pay attention to this too. We get testosterone pumping by working out and lifting weights. I find you get better results if you look in the mirror while doing this. You can get a better perspective of the "before" and "after." You probably think I'm referring to a muscular difference, but I am in fact talking about "before" the testosterone kicks in and "after" the testosterone kicks in. For those of you who didn't know it, testosterone actually has a distinct characteristic when there are sudden increases in it. These characteristics typically reveal themselves in the facial region, but can sometimes show up in other areas as well.

The facial region signals are pretty obvious. Sudden increases in testosterone levels generally result in a dipping and quivering of the lower left lip. This is coupled with the automatic squinting of the left eye. Alternative facial coloration is another key factor. Reddish / purplish is my usual color when those increases come along. If you can, go to a mirror and mimic these facial descriptions so you can see what sudden increased levels in testosterone look like. It isn't always pretty, but there you go.

Other areas of the body give indicators for this sudden increase in testosterone as well. For example, the arms may give way to road maps of veins that were non-existent before the testosterone increase. You may also see immediate, increased perspiration, not only in the arms but in other areas of the body as well. Some like to call this sweat, but I believe it is the muscles actually crying. You may also witness involuntary twitching in places you didn't realize could actually move. The lungs also give off indicators of sudden increases in testosterone. The two big ones are giving off a sudden release that sounds like a bear trying to call for a doctor, and the immediate inability to replenish that sudden release. This makes it difficult to oxygenate the bloodstream, which only increases the physicality of the initial effects of the higher testosterone levels.

As I mentioned earlier, not always pretty. We men do pay attention, though, and look for the ways to have the appropriate increase in testosterone. Our "after" look takes some getting used to. Another relevant topic in the area of testosterone levels is the topic of sex. I believe I have finally figured out a way to help women understand men's sex drive and how to relate to it.

As mentioned in an earlier chapter, men tend to think about sex a little more often than women. From a procreation point of view, it only makes sense to have testosterone want to "spread its seed" for the sake of the human race. I don't think women always understand the true power of this drive, and the effects it has on us. We have already discussed things men can and will do just to increase their chances to have sex. What is important here is to understand why we do it. Please consider this hypothesis. If you are a woman, imagine a time in your life that you were really in the mood, and I mean REALLY in the mood. This may have been because of a dry spell, or a hormonal shift, or you just watched a Brad Pitt movie. The point I am making is that you are REALLY in the mood. Take that feeling, that drive, that wanting, and multiply it by 1,000. That is how most of us men feel at our "low" point. So you can only imagine how we feel at our "high" point. It is very powerful and very commanding. We do our best to channel that power into something good, but without the proper outlet, it usually just ends up in the fast driving or the bar fights.

So, men, I challenge you, come up with some material that helps women understand the true power of testosterone. Maybe with a little education, empathy, and understanding, we could actually work things into our favor. Of course, it could also potentially be manipulated, too, but I'm sure the chances of that are very small, right?

Emotions:

This is both an easy one and a hard one for you women to figure out. The easy part is the understanding that men don't have anywhere near the spectrum of emotional variation women have. That being said, our indicators for emotional change are pretty much non-existent. To women's credit, their emotional outlet is a pretty good indicator as to what they are feeling. If a woman cries, she is sad or upset. She smiles, she is happy. Her face is sour with dipped eyebrows, you are in trouble. Fairly transparent most of the time. The only real trouble is trying to figure out what caused a particular emotion(s) in the first place.

The trouble with men is that when it comes to emotions, we are primarily expressionless. Our happy face pretty much looks the same as our sad face. This can pose a real problem for women trying to figure out a man's emotional state at a particular point in time. If a man wants to know the emotional state of another man (which rarely happens), he would just ask. Women, however, don't ever do this because it would be too simple. So women will merely tell the man what emotional state he should be in. Sometimes it will be very direct, "Aren't you happy that I didn't make you clean the garage today?" Ironically, he suddenly is happy despite what his previous emotion was. After all, he didn't have to clean the garage today (what he doesn't know is that this is usually a psychological trick to guilt him into doing it tomorrow. After all, you didn't have to do it yesterday). Other times, the emotional manipulation will be more subtle. A situation might look something like this…

Woman: "Would you mind putting this dish away?"

Man: (who for all practical purposes is on cloud nine having the best day of his life, and is exemplifying it by putting on his happy face, which looks just like his sad face) "Sure thing."

Woman: "Anything you want to talk about?"

Man: (now confused and wondering if there is something that he is forgetting or is supposed to talk about) "What do you mean, like about what?"

Woman: "Oh, I don't know, you've just seemed a little distant lately, and I was wondering if there was anything bothering you?"

Man: (now wondering how he has been distant, and then suddenly side kicked with an opposing force to his previous state of utopia) "Uh, I don't know."

Woman: "Well, just know that if there is anything bothering you, that you can always talk to me about it, I am here for you."

Man: (who was previously going to go chop some wood, mow the lawn, wrestle a bear and conquer the world, but is now going to go to the basement and watch some mindless television) "Oh, okay."

It's no big secret that women can do this to us, but let's address the main issue here. There is no need for women to control or exercise men's emotions. We do have them, and if you want to know what they are, just ask. In most cases, we will be happy to share them with you. Just don't be confused when you interpret that happiness as our "sad" face. Although it may be short, someone should write more about men's emotions. Just hurry up and do it before you are asked if anything is bothering you.

Fight or flight:

The fight or flight response has been very important to human survival. Back in the day, you ran across a tiger in the forest, and you chose to either fight or run. Adrenaline kicked in, and you all of a sudden possessed superhuman strength. If you used that superhuman strength to run, or "flight," then you lived to run or fight another day. If you used that superhuman strength to "fight" a tiger, then more than likely as you are reading this, you are not an offspring of that individual.

This response has served us well for survival over the years. Today our likelihood of running across a tiger is relatively minimal. Living in a society, with laws, we are able to walk around in safety most of the time. If we do find ourselves exercising the fight or flight response, it is oftentimes on a relative scale.

Keep in mind, as men, our DNA is hardwired to deal with this fight or flight response regardless of the severity of the situation. If we are walking down a dark alley at 2:00 in the morning and we are robbed at gunpoint, then the response kicks in. Our physiological response is to either handle the situation to the best of our ability, or get out of there as quickly as we can. Seemingly, very appropriate.

The problem comes in when we have this response to slightly less severe situations. For example, we have a dirty sock waved in front of our face with an agitated comment such as "Haven't I told you eight times just this week to put your dirty clothes in the laundry?" Although this "attack" isn't that threatening, our body and mind can't really differentiate. Our fight or flight response kicks in. Therefore, we either punch our "attacker" in the face, or we retreat to some place where we can be alone (and seemingly safe). Since punching women in the face goes against the code of *most* men, we tend to just retreat.

It is my belief this is where we derive the need for our "man cave." In the man cave, we can at least feel safe and do no wrong, even if it is just for a little while. The man cave is also a place where we are free from "extra" sounds. We are not only free from extra sounds, we are also free from extra activities, extra items, and extra smells. Believe it or not, many men are not a fan of "extra" most of the time. We like things simple, and the man cave is where we can get it.

The things men like to do in their man caves depends on the individual. However, it is my belief that they have all formed out of this "flight" response to relatively non-threatening situations. The challenge I propose is that someone out there write some material for what all goes on in the man cave. I'm sure many women would benefit from having a greater understanding of not only the activities, but the need for this retreat. Most importantly, ladies, if you want/need us around for something, please make sure you don't initiate the fight or flight response. Maybe just pick up the sock, and then wait to tell us about it when there is a time you *don't* want us around. I can't imagine when that would ever be.

Money and what it's for:

As mentioned earlier, we typically only buy things we don't intend to return. Returning items for men is not only more/redundant work, but also a sign of indecisiveness, which commonly doesn't sit well with us.

To remain consistent with previous chapters, we will acknowledge that on a basic level men will buy things that are either loud, heavy, ugly, and/or shiny. There are, of course, other items that will fall outside of these parameters. For example, beer does not really fit into any of these categories, but we will buy it. I suppose one could make the argument that if you buy enough of it that it would be heavy, but other than that, it's in a category by itself.

On the flip side, a man will purchase something that fits into all of these categories. For example, we can buy a firearm. The best firearm is loud, heavy, ugly, and shiny. Oftentimes we buy things that fit just a couple of the categories, like our favorite arm chair. Either way, we keep our money uses relatively simple.

Our money spending probably doesn't make a lot of sense to most women. I know for myself, I will spend a lot of money to improve something that was working just fine in the first place. As we have discussed in earlier chapters, a lot of this will circle around electronics. It can always be louder. I state it unapologetically, because there are money spending scenarios from women that I don't understand either. Again, these differences are simply differences. It's okay if we don't understand them, they are what they are. As long as there is a roof over our head, food on the table, and clothes on our back (that haven't been returned, of course), then all should be good.

On the subject of things being returned, this is the one area where men actually get a little bit back in the time department. If you calculated all the time that women spend on returning items, we might actually be in a breakeven scenario when it comes to "multitasking" versus "non-multitasking." So what this does is gives us one more variable to solve for comparing "male mathematics" and "female mathematics." We will call this variable Z, which is represented by *time spent returning purchased items*. Let's look at some equations based off of these variables, which I will redefine so that you are not confused....

$$Z = \text{time women spend returning items}$$

$$X = \text{time men spend trying to save time}$$

$$Y = \text{actual time men save}$$

In review, we have these previously proven equations....

$$Y=2X \qquad \text{and} \qquad 1 \geq 2$$

…..and now we have…

$$X=Z$$

…therefore we can further break down the equation to look something like this…

$$\frac{Y}{1} \geq \frac{2(x \text{ or } z)}{2}$$

…or by dividing out the 2 on the right side of the equation we have…

$$\frac{Y}{1} \geq X \text{ or } Z$$

After we break this down, you might be asking yourself *"so what does this tell us?"* And the simplest answer is that it should be clear that I didn't do all that well in college algebra. It indeed does require a bit of work to figure this out, and may not bear the highest level of relevance. However, it does signify that what I really should have spent *my* money on was a math tutor.

To sum up, it is clear to see that I have only touched on some of the areas that both men and women need better and further education on. I again challenge you to identify your own relevant topics of education, and get the word out. My life is already in danger for publishing this book, so if you want to send it to me to get the word out, just send it to info@womantalkbook.com. I will be happy to share your information and keep you safe.

As usual, men are a little easier to calculate when it comes to expanding our education and understanding about them. Women can be a little trickier. I will sometimes argue that women like to mess with men simply because they can. Nothing solidifies that point more than a situation that occurred with my daughter and my son. We were flying to Prague to visit my wife's family, and we were fairly early on in our 22-hour "door to door" travel. My daughter (Klara) had her turn next to the window (a level of fairness that needs constant monitoring). My son (Kalvin), already upset that he is not next to the window, attempted to look out as best as he can from the seat next to her. Klara, and her little 4 year old "woman" mind, noticed this.

There were essentially two windows that could be used for viewing pleasure from our particular spot on the plane that trip. One window Klara was comfortably sitting back and looking out of, the other Kalvin was leaning forward and trying to see as best as he could. Klara noticed he was trying to look out of this forward window, so she decided she was going to lean forward and look out of this window herself and block his view.

This is the point where I simply expected my son to lose it. I was pleasantly surprised when I saw his little 5 year old mind search for a solution as he leaned back and looked as best as he could from the window that Klara had moved from. In a utopian world, that is where this story would have ended. In a "Woman Talk" world, this is where it just begins. Klara sees that Kalvin has switched windows for his viewing pleasure, and decides that this did not frustrate him nearly as much as she wanted so she goes back to her original window. Kalvin (in another proud father moment) simply leans back forward to look out of his original window as well.

Again, if the story ended there then all would still be good. Klara, however, would not be satisfied until she got under his skin. So using her large range of vision, she is now simply getting in front of Kalvin no matter which window he is looking out of. She moves forward, he moves back. Then she moves back, and he moves forward. This goes on for about ten times. It looked like they are trying to get a "wave" started that no one else wanted to participate in. Finally, Kalvin lost it and complained to mom and dad. We, of course, had already been watching the whole situation in amazement and needed no briefing on the matter. I looked into my daughter's eyes, and in my stern, fatherly, bass filled voice informed her that she was to pick one window to look out of and not move from that spot. Case closed, problem solved. Yeah, right!

My daughter decided to choose her original window, as it was most comfortable in the first place. She also decided to listen to daddy and not move from that spot. What she also did though, was close the visor on the window that brother was looking out of. He lost it again. I informed her (with my fatherly voice again) that she is to open that visor immediately if she knows what's good for her. She complied by opening the visor, making this now her window of choice, and closing the visor on the original window that she was looking out of. Now she has both her brother and her father losing it (I'm sure she could not be more pleased). At this point, all I could do was stare at her and give her a final "KLARA", to which she knew meant she should sit in her seat, not move, and keep both visors the same. Only problem is, she decided to close both of them.

Rather than get upset, I simply looked at my wife and said "YOU are going to have hard time with her in about 9 years." The gentleman sitting behind us started laughing and said "That's the exact same thing I told my wife about our daughter." If this situation does not clearly define that women like to sometimes mess with men simply because they can, then nothing will define it. No amount of understanding or education can prepare you for a situation like this.

That being said, what would make me happiest would be if we were able to better equip our formal education process to include some of this highly relevant information. It is true that we will never understand how to prepare for the situation previously mentioned, but I think we could make some real progress if we revamped some of the course topics currently available to us.

For example, instead of teaching "Economics," we could formalize a class called "Female Mathematics" so we would understand how money really works (you might want to sell any stock you have in Excedrin before this course is offered, its use will probably go way down). We could add more relevance to topics like "History" if we understood "You're History if you don't give me some time for my nails." Instead of courses like general "Communications," we could have "Communications" relevant to communicating with the opposite sex. Statistics could be taught in a way that would help us understand how success in a relationship of the opposite sex is almost impossible (at least we would know it). English, well that opens up all kinds of options for courses if we truly want to understand each other. This "real" education on these "real" topics would almost have to catapult our successes in dealing with and understanding the opposite sex. If nothing else, men could finally "save time" by knowing when to give up.

Chapter 9
...In The End.

So now that we've gotten through decrypting all this information, let me summarize the optimal way for the opposite sexes to truly understand and relate to each other:

Stop trying.

Yes, my advice is to give up. However, if you wish to try, then let's review. Understand these differences as what they are, innate differences between the sexes and try to be light-hearted and humorous about them – you'll live longer. We'll never think like each other, even if we wanted to try. Just understand that we are different, and attempt to appreciate the other's perspective.

Let me once again summarize with a few words/rules that will help you interpret the differences between men and women. You will undoubtedly recognize some of these, and if you don't, then by all means this is your homework (These were jokes shared with me via the internet/email, no original author was found).

Words women use and what they really mean:

Fine: This is the word women use to end an argument when they feel they are right and you need to shut up. Never use fine to describe how a woman looks. This will cause you to have one of those arguments.

Five Minutes: This is half an hour. It is equivalent to the five minutes that your football game is going to last before you take out the trash, so it's an even trade.

Nothing: This means something, and you should be on your toes. Nothing is usually used to describe the feeling a woman has of wanting to turn you inside out, upside down, and backwards. Nothing usually signifies an argument that will last Five Minutes and end up with the word Fine.

Go Ahead (with eyebrows raised): This is a dare. One that will result in a woman getting upset over Nothing, and will end with the word Fine.

Go Ahead (normal eyebrows): This means, I give up, or do what you want because I don't care. You will get a Raised Eyebrow Go Ahead in just a few minutes, followed by Nothing and Fine, and she will talk to you in Five Minutes when she cools off.

Loud Sigh: This is not actually a word, but is a nonverbal statement often misunderstood by men. A Loud Sigh means she thinks you are an idiot at that moment, and wonders why she is wasting her time standing here and arguing with you over Nothing.

Soft Sigh: Again, not a word, but a nonverbal statement. Soft Sighs mean that she is content. Your best bet is not to move or breathe, and she will stay content.

That's Okay: This is one of the most dangerous statements a woman can make to a man. That's Okay means that she wants to think long and hard before paying you back for whatever it is that you have done. That's Okay is often used with the word Fine and in conjunction with a Raised Eyebrow Go Ahead. At some point in the near future, you are going to be in some mighty big trouble.

Please Do: This is not a statement, it is an offer. A woman is giving you the chance to come up with whatever excuse or reason you have for doing whatever it is that you have done. You have a fair chance with the truth, so be careful and you shouldn't get a That's Okay.

Thanks: A woman is thanking you. Do not faint, just say you're welcome.

Thanks A Lot: This is much different from Thanks. A woman will say Thanks A Lot when she is really ticked off at you. It signifies that you have offended her in some callous way, and will be followed by the Loud Sigh. Be careful not to ask what is wrong after the Loud Sigh, as she will only tell you Nothing.

Now, let's take a look at the how the other side works. Men typically like to work their lives around "rules." This shouldn't be too surprising, with all that we have learned throughout this book. So women, pay attention here. If you can understand these rules, then everyone's life will be better.

Men's Rules:

Crying is blackmail.

Ask what you want: Let us be clear on this one, subtle hints don't work, strong hints don't work, obvious hints don't work. Just say it.

"Yes" and "No" are perfectly acceptable answers to almost every question.

Come to us with a problem only if you want help solving it: That's what we do. Sympathy and listening is what your girlfriends are for.

Anything we said six months ago is inadmissible in an argument: In fact, all comments become null and void after seven days.

You can either "ask" us to do something, or "tell" us how you want it done, not both: If you already know best how to do it, just do it yourself.

So there you have it. "Words" and "Rules" that further solidify what I have been saying since "In The Beginning." Kind of funny when you look at it this way. So leave out the big problems, leave out the assault and battery. Just identify these as never changing, ironic little differences between men and women.

My wife has been kind enough to always give me an "out" when it comes to things that she expects from me. She has solidified low expectations by adopting the phrase "You're just a man." At first, I took offense to this statement. That was my ego invested young self. Now that I am older, I welcome this statement with open arms. Also, I am in a comfortable enough position where I don't have to take advantage of that statement. We have passionately adopted and implemented our Core Values in our household (discussed further in the next chapter). Truth be told, if you love each other, respect each other, communicate with each other, and care about each other, then you can't go wrong. Maybe they should change the song to "all you need is love, respect, communication, and caring." I suppose that may not sell as many records.

We all have our challenges in any relationship that we have. I find it truly sad, however, to think of an amount of time, or a set of circumstances that would change you from wanting the very best for your partner. If you ever start to feel this way, take a step back and try to remember the things that made you fall in love in the first place. Refuel those things, and bring the passion and the wanting back into your life and your relationship. Remember that, within reason, there isn't anything you can't do.

I recently attended the wedding of a friend of my wife's. About half way through the ceremony, the minister stopped talking to the couple, and started talking to those of us in the audience. He was reminding us on how to get through the troubled times, when things aren't perfect. As I was listening, I was taken back fourteen years earlier (to the month) and reminded of my own wedding. I remember the minister who married us asking what he called a "trick" question before we got married. He asked each of us if we would still love the other in ten years if the same person was sitting across from us then. We, of course, both answered "no," knowing that in ten years we would have hopefully grown to be different people. As I reflected back on that moment, I was thrilled to discover that I love my wife far more today than I did fourteen years ago. We were both very different people back then, and while I liked both of them, they do not compare to who we are today and the relationship that is before us now. I am excited about what another fourteen years will bring.

I have a sincere appreciation for what my wife, Lida, does for me, for our children, for family and friends, and for herself. Truth be told, I feel as if I'm the luckiest guy in the world. I thank you for having an interest in reading this book, and I hope you have learned something from it.

Best of luck in your application of the Code "Woman Talk," the now "decrypted" language that women never wanted men to know.

Chapter 10
Bonus Chapter: Strategic Happiness

Concepts and information in this chapter were originally within the other chapters of this book. However, after feedback and analysis, I thought it was best to put it at the end of the book as a bonus chapter. There are two main reasons for this decision. The first is that the subject matter is quite a bit less humorous than the rest of the book. The second reason is that the subject matter strays just a little.

The main focus of this bonus chapter centers around strategies for being happy. This includes strategies for men and women as couples and individuals. It is a compilation of strategies and principles that I have learned and implemented in my own life. I felt that it was selfish not to share them with you. However, if you would like to end this book on the comical, humorous tone that the rest of the book hopefully provided, then you will in no way hurt my feelings if you choose not to read on. If you do choose to read on, then I humbly offer my tools for success and happiness, and hope that you get as much out of them that I have. Enjoy.

In college I took a business course that dealt with a concept of TQM, or Total Quality Management. This concept centers around the philosophy that things can continue to improve, and with proper focus they will. I've always loved that idea, and I work to implement that same philosophy into my own life. That being said, I'm going to get a little serious on you here for a minute (I know, crazy huh?), and share with you some different books that have made a tremendous impact on my life over the years.

Now I'm going to warn you and remind you that my degree is in Business Administration, and that's a strong area of interest for me. Therefore, many of the readings I relate to here will center loosely, if not directly, around business. It is my opinion, however, that many of the same qualities in business relationships are also applicable in relationships between men and women. Take what you like and what is relevant, and discard the rest.

The first book that made a profound difference in my life is *The 7 Habits of Highly Effective People* by Dr. Stephen R. Covey. If you haven't read this, I highly encourage you to do so. In fact, read it, reread it, digest it, and live it. As you read, take the time to do any exercise that it asks as you to do. This will help you really own the concepts addressed. This is one of my favorite books because its principles can be used in business, in friendship, in marriage, and many other relationships.

One favorite issue this book raises for me is the desire to "victimize" ourselves from time to time that all of us seem to have. Some more than others. Dr. Covey addresses the reasons for this behavior in his first Habit – Be Proactive. No, this isn't a skin-cleaning habit, but rather is the habit of taking charge and being responsible for ourselves. The reason we tend to want to victimize ourselves is because it absolves us of responsibility on a particular issue, and allows us to blame external forces for the "reason" for our circumstances.

This may sound a little crazy, but we all do it to some degree. In fact, you may not recognize to what degree until you start to focus on it. I often say that "what you focus on grows," good or bad, so by all means make it good. Dr. Covey gives a brilliant visual in what he calls the Circle of Influence and Circle of Concern. The main premise is to focus on the things you can control, and not give blame to the things you can't.

The second favorite topic that comes to mind is what Dr. Covey describes in Habit 3: Put First Things First, as in "The Time Management Matrix." In it, he prioritizes activities as being either important or not important, and urgent or not urgent. The key is to spend as much time on "important but not urgent" activities as possible. He does a wonderful job at giving analogies and situations we all can relate to.

The reason these two topics are favorites of mine is they consistently come up when I talk to people about problems. Both the Habits of "Be Proactive" and "Put First Things First" are in what Dr. Covey calls the "Private Victory" section of his book. I believe it is an area of our lives that even if we have a good handle on it, we can continue to improve (TQM). How easy is it to blame a spouse for your own personal shortcomings in a particular area? Does that blame fix the problem? Does that blame strengthen or weaken the relationship? When we put it in black and white, it seems obvious. However, we're all human and unless we're making a conscious effort, then we shouldn't be surprised by the results. Only a fool would complain about where the current has taken him, while never dipping his paddle in the water.

The second of my favorite books is *Laws of Success* by Napoleon Hill. It was originally written by Mr. Hill in the earlier part of the 1900s, and is a study in the key principles/laws that make successful people successful. Over his 25-year study, he found principles/laws that were consistent in all of the people he studied. Ironically enough, I have read where Dr. Covey was highly influenced by the work of Napoleon Hill. No surprise I like both of their works.

I highly encourage you to digest this book. As an older book, the more recent editions give comparisons and analogies to more recent situations and companies (which I think is nice), but I'm sure any edition is good. Just to give you an idea of the topics, I am going to name the chapters in my edition so you can see the book's focus. As you read through the 17 chapter titles, think about how they might relate to you and your situation…..

Introduction to the Master Mind

A Definite Chief Aim

Self-Confidence

The Habit of Saving

Initiative and Leadership

Imagination

Enthusiasm

Self-Control

The Habit of Doing More Than Getting Paid For

A Pleasing Personality

Accurate Thinking

Concentration

Cooperation

Profiting by Failure

Tolerance

The Golden Rule

The Universal Law of Cosmic Habitforce

    As I mentioned, the concepts and philosophies behind these principles/laws were consistent throughout all of the people Mr. Hill studied. We're talking about people such as Andrew Carnegie, Henry Ford, and Thomas Edison, to name a few.
    If you haven't read these books, I encourage you to take the time to read them. I can honestly say they made a tremendous positive impact on my life. The beautiful thing is they address "principles" that are relevant under many different situations and topics. That makes them easy to discuss with many people, in all of our varieties.
    In my search for knowledge in college, the best thing I learned was to always continue to search for knowledge. I'm not sure college was the most cost-effective way to come to this realization, but there it is. I think lots of people go to college for the wrong reasons nowadays. I remember a business communications course I had in college, where a local businessperson came in to talk about the interviewing process (I won't mention the company). Since I worked in theater management at the time, and since I interviewed lots of people, I was anxious to see what I could learn and add to my interviewing skills, something I took seriously.

In college, I learned to always sit in the front row in the center. I found this was the best place to sit to enhance the learning process. I also discovered this was the only seat that I could stay awake in if I found the subject matter particularly uninteresting. So there I sat as the individual came in to discuss the interviewing process, and how to conduct a good interview. The individual opened with her name, the company she was from, and then proceeded to ask "How many of you are here because you want to make more money?" I chose not to raise my hand, but after she looked at me rather curiously, I happened to catch a glance at the rest of the class behind me. They all had their hands up. This person then addressed the fact that I was the only one who didn't have my hand raised.

"You didn't raise your hand," she said to me, sounding almost insulted. I replied, "That's because that's not the reason that I'm here." Her frustration continued as she asked me in a condescending tone, "Well, why are you here?" I replied, "I'm here to get an education. If that's wrong, then I apologize." I swear you could almost see her foot go into her mouth. She hurriedly waved the matter off and went right into talking about interviewing. I think it should go without saying that I wasn't impressed.

Which brings me back to my point, I think sometimes we go to college for the wrong reasons. Sure, more money may be the end result (certainly not guaranteed) of a higher education, but that shouldn't be the goal. I believe our goal is to have a well-rounded education, and in my case, it taught me to always work toward continuing that education. More importantly, not only get an education, but work toward applying the knowledge we learn. With today's technology, we have an increasingly large amount of information readily available to us at almost any given point in time. Deciphering it seems to often be a problem. It's important to identify the areas in life you want to be educated.

Humor me for just a moment and really think about that statement. Take five minutes (probably even less) and put pen to paper and list the items in "life" you feel it is important to be educated in. Put another way, write down the areas in life that tend to have universal importance to everyone in their lives. Think of it as different slices of a whole pie, that in total make up the major areas of focus and importance in your life. Do it now, then come back. I'll wait.

Really, do it now, don't just keep reading, do it now.

So how did you do? Did you find that exercise easy or difficult? It more than likely depends on how much you've thought about this before. Whether it was easy or difficult doesn't matter, what matters is that you did it. Having done it, you should now have a baseline (if you didn't before) for every decision that is in front of you, and a defined purpose.

Your "pie" can look something like this, depending on how many areas of importance you came up with.....

Pie of Importance

We'll call this the "Pie of Importance." You may have more slices or fewer slices in yours, and that's fine. The important thing is that you have a Pie. You may find that if you sit down with a group of people and do this exercise, you'll have similar answers. The sum of the parts of our Pie should form what you consider to be "happiness." After all, this should really be the goal for all of us. We want to be happy. We want our children to be happy. The problem often is that if we forget this is the goal, then we get sidetracked by all of the variables in life. Ignore the variables, and get back to your Pie of Importance.

The five *main* areas in my life that make up the pieces of my Pie are Family, Friends, Health, Financial Security, and Spiritual Fulfillment. This may be similar to your list, or it may not. Either way is perfectly fine. However, these are the areas that demand the attention in my life, and those who share their lives with me. Your Pie may have different sized slices of Pie; this way you can allocate a "percentage of importance" within your important areas. All of these together, however, should be used to define your *Core Values* that help you make decisions in all areas of your life.

As mentioned earlier, *Variables* in life can distract us from what our goals and areas of importance are. These variables come in many different forms. The problem is, if we haven't defined our Core Values, then these *Variable Values* can temporarily take on the role of a Core Value. They can't sustain that position, for they will eventually end up conflicting with another variable value. In much the same way we addressed the "Variable Factor" in Chapter 3, we can see that by juggling these Variable Values around, we can work things to never have the "right answer." Unfortunately, this can quickly become evident in our home, professional, and social lives.

If we constantly operate from a Core Value perspective though, we will quickly re-adjust and know we're making the best decisions to meet our goals, without conflict from other Variable Values.

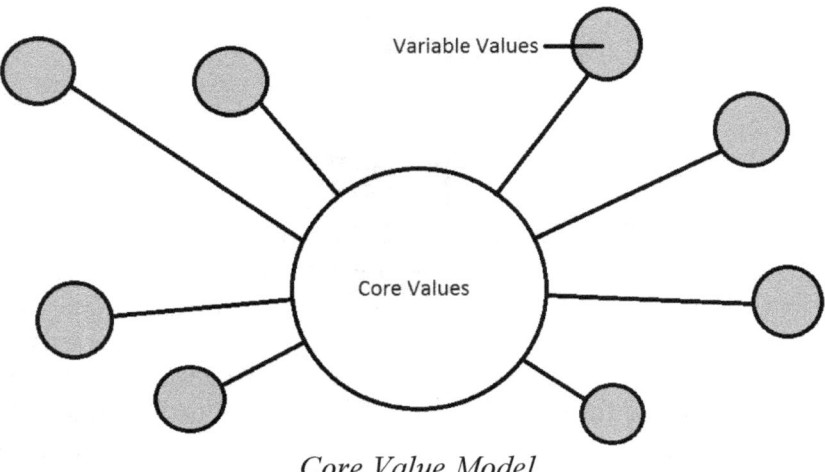

Core Value Model

(You always have to come back to your Core Values before working on or defining any Variable Values.)

Your success with a spouse will depend on how much these individual Core Values align with each other. The more these values align, the easier the marriage will be. The more at odds they are, the harder it will be. One of the best things you can do to encourage the success of a marriage is to figure this out before the marriage. That, however, is practical, logical, and anti-romantic, so it's rarely done. Along with these Core Values, it's a good idea to communicate your needs and wants with a spouse. Some of you may laugh at me (my wife does), but I have a Personal Mission Statement that helps communicate those wants and needs. This concept aligns very nicely with the Core Value Model because it brings to light the important areas that demand our focus in our lives.

I developed this Personal Mission Statement several years ago with the online assistance of the Franklin Covey Institute. It has served as a very helpful resource and guide in all of the Core Value areas of my life. My Personal Mission Statement is, as it says, personal, but I am willing to share it with you here because of how tremendously helpful and important it has been. Here it is.

Life is defined in many different ways by many different people. Philosophers, theologians, and many others have contemplated life and its meaning since the dawn of time. The following Mission Statement is not an attempt to define, theorize, or hypothesize the meaning of life. Rather, it is a statement that serves as a guide to find Happiness, Fulfillment, and Value in the living of my own life.

- I will **Lead** a life centered around principles that are important to me. These principles include Integrity, Patience, Fairness, and Human Dignity. I will apply these principles to all areas of my life that require attention.

- I will **Remember** and find Balance in my life within the areas that are most important to me. These areas of importance are Family, Friends, Health, Financial Security, and Spiritual Fulfillment. These areas take precedence over anything else concerning decisions that affect my life and those in it.

- I will **Revere** admirable characteristics in others, such as being Ambitious, Proactive, Enthusiastic, Dependable, Principle-Centered, and Fairness. I will also attempt to implement similar characteristics in my own life.

- I will **Recognize** my Strengths and develop talents as a person who is Open-Minded, Reliable, a Teacher, Practical, Adaptable, and Kind.

- I will **Humble** myself by acknowledging that I can be Fearful, Pessimistic, and a Procrastinator. I will constantly strive to transform these Weaknesses and any others into Strengths.

- I will Envision myself becoming a person who finds Balance in the important areas of my life. In the areas of my **Marriage**, I will constantly be open to and support life decisions that Lida will experience as our marriage matures. I will be Caring, Fun, and Sensitive to her needs, my needs, and Our needs. I will recognize our marriage for the asset that it is, and that is a Loving and Synergistic entity, whose whole is far greater than the sum of its parts. With my **Family** and **Friends**, I will strive to be Respectful, Responsible, Sensitive and Trustworthy, and at the same time be Light and Fun. In the areas of my **Profession** and **Teaching**, I will act in accordance with being Dependable, Committed, Organized, and Sincere. While these general areas of my life sometimes require differences, I will continually **Strive** for and **Envision** myself Balancing these differences to become a person who satisfies the needs and wants of those whom are important in my life.

While this Personal Mission Statement serves as a Guide, I will constantly review it and not use it as a map. As roads, cities, and rivers change, I understand that so do the walks of life. I will be open to changes in my life that might redefine success in Happiness, Fulfillment, and the Value of living, and make adjustments accordingly.

This Personal Mission Statement is what serves as a guide to remind me of my Core Values. As we all know, life is full of distractions that try to "knock us off track," so this brings me back every time. I highly encourage you to make one for yourself (if you haven't already), and to put it in a place that you can refer to it often, preferably every day.

So now I would like to share with you my different slices of Pie, and share what education and focus is important in each area. I am confident these are sound principles. Mainly because I am one of the happiest people I know. That being said, remember to take what you want, and discard the rest. We have looked at some of the many humorous differences between the male and female gender. If they're not kept in check, they can become no longer humorous but a serious drain on us, our spouse, our kids, even our friends. So let's "slice this Pie up," and see if we can give some *focus* on what makes these pieces taste the best.

Family and Friends

I am going to go ahead and put these two together because fortunately for me they are one and the same. I am fortunate to have family as friends, and friends as family, if that makes sense. Family and friends can be your biggest assets or your biggest liabilities. Fortunately, you can choose your friends. Family can be a little trickier.

Call it cliché, but you are who you hang around with. Knowing that, hang around with people you want to be like. I remember once reading something that said, "The answer to the question in life is not to find yourself, but design yourself." I believe there is a lot of truth to that statement. Choose friends wisely. Choose friends who will be happy about your growth and accomplishments, and reciprocate it with being happy about theirs.

Far too often we are caught up with petty feelings like jealousy, envy, and sabotage (including self-sabotage). We fall into comfort zones of mediocrity, and try to keep others there, too, so we can be "comfortable" with our own existence. This is not true family or true friendship.

We are all guilty of this on some level. If you don't believe me, try this short exercise. Imagine a friend of yours who has maybe struggled a little. A good friend, but someone who maybe you've tried to help out, with maybe little or no show of appreciation. Now, imagine that friend just won the lottery. Are you happy for that person? Are you maybe a little envious, a little jealous? It's only natural. This example may be on the far end of the bell curve, but I want you to understand the situation is there. More than likely, it would take far less than this extreme example to conjure up these feelings.

I am fortunate to have both friends that I chose, and also to have the family that I do, and to be truly happy for them in their successes. If anyone in my circle won the lottery, I would truly be happy for them. This has capitalized on what I like to call the "four percent" that I both choose and have been blessed to surround myself with. I say the term "four percent" to refer to a scenario that a small group of friends and myself have come to understand. While the math isn't exactly correct, it still drives home a valid point that goes something like this. If I made a life change/accomplishment, say bought a brand new car just as an example. Forty-eight percent of people have a better car than me and don't give a damn. Forty-eight percent of people will be jealous of this purchase and be envious of me. Four percent of people will be *truly happy* for my accomplishment and reaching that dream/goal. Make that four percent your friends.

Family can be a little trickier. You can't really choose your family. It's important to identify and recognize your family for what it is. A family can mean different things to different people. Much of this is probably dependent upon the age and stage of life of a particular individual. So it's important to ask yourself "what is family." Just by answering this question you can create a basic baseline for *yourself* on what role family will take. Some of you might be thinking of your spouse and your kids. Others of you might be thinking of your parents and your siblings. Still others of you might be thinking about your kids and your grandkids. Family can be any one or all of these scenarios, and everything in between.

A key component is to identify what you count on family for. If you are a child, you count on your parents to feed you, clothe you, love you, and educate you. You are entirely dependent upon your parents for everything that Maslow defined in his hierarchy of needs (see a graphic of Maslow's hierarchy below). Your Core Values pretty much have to align with theirs to some degree, for good or bad.

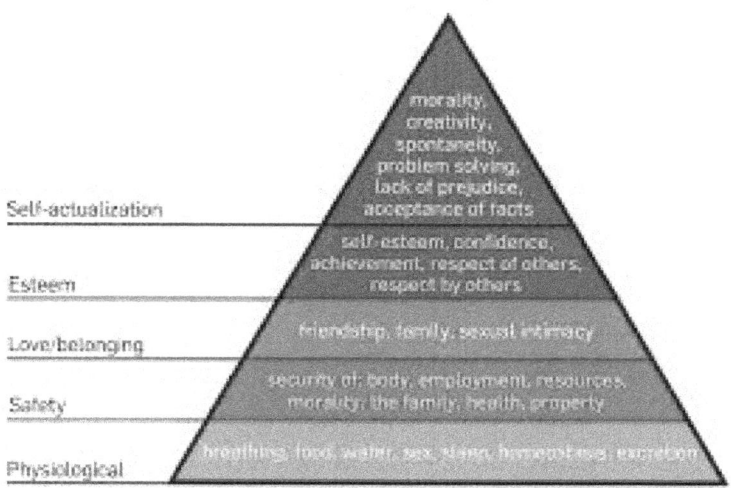

This can be good or bad for the child, good if there are good Core Values from the Parents, bad if there are bad Core Values from the parents (incredibly relative, of course). As a child, even a defiant child, I think there is an underlying thought process that your parents know what's best. Even though it's in your nature to resist this concept sometimes, in a "bell curve" scenario you think to yourself that *"Mom and Dad knows best."* I never understood, until the day that I became a parent, how far from the truth this is.

Of course, we're speaking again in terms of relativity. That being said, I felt pretty comfortable with what I knew and what I was doing before my first child was born. My son's birth "rocked my world" as far as shaking that comfort up. Here we were, in our mid-thirties, after being married for eight years, careers established, and what a game changer our son's birth was. Truth be told, I realized I didn't know shit.

My parents had been married for maybe a couple of years and had me in their early twenties. I quickly realized how much less they must have known than I did, and I have to give them credit for doing an excellent job raising me. Now don't get me wrong, I'm not foolishly giving *all* the credit to them. I put my own decisions and judgments in there as well. However, I was blessed to have a good Core Value baseline to operate from.

That is truly the biggest fear I had when that tiny, new, innocent and magnificent life was born that we called our son. Even if I had the book of "all the right answers" in front of me, he will, both fortunately and unfortunately, have free will. It's a scary thing for those who take raising a child seriously. So stack the deck in your favor by providing that child with good Core Values.

Blending the Family

It's no big secret anymore that there are a lot of unhappy households out there. Divorce rates are the highest ever. The family dynamic is becoming increasingly more complicated. This poses a real challenge for providing solid and "consistent" Core Values. I stress consistent here because, as mentioned earlier, Core Values can be relative. There is no "book of right answers" out there because there are no right answers. There are only perspective and relativity. Sure, many of us fit in the bell curve, but there are differences in the bell curve even outside of the extremes.

As strong of an asset as values are, they can serve as a liability too. The main reason being that if someone argues directly against your values, right or wrong, you pretty much consider them an enemy. Slight differences can be healthy at providing perspective, but stray too much off the line and you can have some real problems. If someone argues with you that 2+2=6, you are going to have a very difficult time accepting that one (unless you are calculating an advanced mathematical formula via the "Female Mathematics" method from Chapter 2). Still, it's easy to see why strong Core Values can "make or break" a family relationship. Let's take a look at both sides of that scenario (very simplified).

A man and woman meet and fall in love. They fall in love because they met in similar circles, they were attracted to one another, and they felt they had a lot in common. Upon sitting down and evaluating their Core Values, we find they're very much in line. They are in line because the husband came from a family that had and focused on good Core Values, and the wife came from a similar situation. So the husband and wife see eye to eye on what is important to them. They develop their "own" set of Core Values as a couple, but the blend is relatively effortless. The wife can relate well to the husband's parents because they can see eye to eye, and the husband to the wife's Parents for the same reasons. This is a strong family that loves, respects, and communicates with each other.

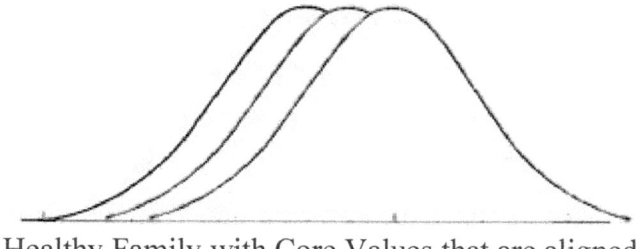

Healthy Family with Core Values that are aligned

Now let's look at another scenario (again, very simplified). A man and a woman meet and fall in love. They fell in love because they met in similar circles, they were attracted to each other, and they *felt* they had a lot in common. Upon sitting down and evaluating their Core Values, we find they are not in line at all. The circles they ran in were a random splattering of individual groups that nomadically wandered through life with no definite plan. The attraction can still exist, but much of that can be explained through animalistic behavior and basic programming to procreate. The husband is a product of his family's bad Core Values. They are primarily bad because they have never been consciously defined, but rather continue to be defined dependent upon the Variable Values that are impeding on their current situation. The wife comes from a similar family situation, and therefore has similarly "situational" defined values. The husband and wife have a hard time defining their "own" set of Core Values because it takes conscious effort, and even with that effort could not be situationally aligned even if they had to.

He cannot relate to her parents; she cannot relate to his. This is a weak family that despises, disrespects, and "talks at" each other.

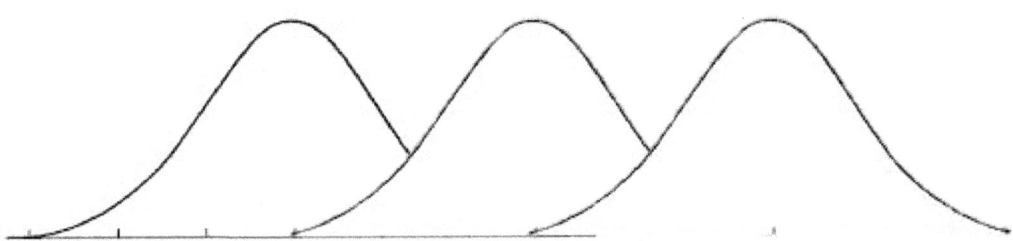

Unhealthy Family with Core Values that are *not* aligned

As you can see, family can be a little trickier. Hopefully, if you're married, you fit more into the first scenario rather than the second. If not, you have some serious assessments to do. If you're yet to be married, consider entering a marriage cautiously. Partners can be our biggest boost or our biggest drain when it comes to life and life situations. That includes all partners -- business, training, and friends. Consider evaluating a potential spouse very carefully when determining your likelihood of success in a relationship. Some would argue "all you need is love," and I would agree with that – In the Beginning.

Health

Physical Health

Health is kind of a funny thing. It is one of the easiest things to take for granted when you have it, and one of the things you most appreciate when you don't. Listing health in my Core Values forces me to acknowledge it on a daily basis.

Health, like many other things, is incredibly relative. I can address this statement with a simple example. You have someone who weighs 225 lbs. Should this person feel good about their weight, should she feel that it is a healthy range? Okay, I know what you're thinking, details right? I'll break it down even more. This person is a female, age 30, and if 5 feet 6 inches tall. How about now? Should she feel good about her size? Most of you are probably thinking no, but here is where the relativity comes in. What if I told you that she used to weigh 600 lbs. Does that change things a bit? Of course, it does. This new weight is much better, and she can consider herself on a path to health, at least compared to how she was before.

So health is relative, but it certainly demands our attention. I say this to help everyone keep things in their proper perspective. Like anything else, we should have wants and dreams and desires, and we should work to attain them. However, it is also important to keep our goals in their proper perspective and not completely "beat ourselves up" if we don't reach them 100%. I am a firm believer in everything in moderation. Health and science journals pertaining to diet will constantly contradict themselves. What is "right" for you today is sure to be "wrong" for you tomorrow. This is the case whether it's related to diet or exercise. My opinion is (and it is only my opinion) that you know you better than anyone does. Listen to yourself and know what your strengths, weaknesses, and limitations are. Understand them, work around them, and take everything in moderation.

One important thing to understand (if you haven't figured this out) is that "diets" don't work. This might sound funny coming from a 150 lb. 40-year-old, but that is exactly my point. "Lifestyles" work, not diets. If your lifestyle is a healthy one, chances are you are going to be healthy. If your lifestyle is an unhealthy one, chances are you are going to be unhealthy. It's really not rocket science.

Does this mean that I have a 100% healthy diet? Absolutely not. We are all human and we all have our vices. However, my vices are "Variables" that tend to stray from the "Core" of my diet. The trick is to keep coming back to the Core.

Hygiene

I know this seems like a basic concept, but when I'm out at different places, it would appear that may not be so basic. There are some places I end up going where the hygienic advice of take a shower at least once a week would seem appropriate, but I'm not going to address that issue here. What I would like to address is how we present ourselves. I had a professor in college who talked to me about test taking. He told me to think in the terms that every time you put your name at the top of a test, to think of it almost as a signature, as a representation of you. He discussed this to emphasize the importance of what we do.

I challenge us all to keep that in mind when it comes to our hygiene. I always challenge myself to understand this principle whenever I go out, anywhere. When I am out of my home, my physical appearance is a representation of me and my family. What does this mean?

When I worked in theater management, I was always known as the "sharp-dressed guy." To this day, I really couldn't tell you what that means. What I do know is that every time I went to work, I made a conscious effort to make sure my physical appearance was good, that my clothes were clean and ironed, and that my tie matched my shirt. I also mixed things up sometimes with jewelry, different glasses, and vests and blazers. Does this mean all my clothes were Armani or Ralph Lauren? Far from it, but they were clean, ironed, presentable, appreciated, and well cared for. They were a representation of me and my attitude toward the job, and I took it seriously.

In late 2001, I started a medical staffing company and ran the office and administration processes out of my home. I wore a suit every day, even during the initial start-up time when I was the only one in the office. This projected an attitude and professionalism in what I did. Even when I was at home alone. When we go out, we should reflect how we want to be perceived. It's not about vanity; it's about self-worth and importance. In my opinion, it should be our goal to be well groomed and presentable, at a minimum. As I mentioned, this doesn't have to mean high-priced items, it just has to mean appreciated and well-cared-for items. I find it incredibly ironic when I go out and see so many people wearing loose fitting "work out" clothes, that haven't looked like they worked out a day in their life. I keep very active, teach martial arts, and very rarely will you ever see me out in apparel that would indicate this. I like to present myself at a high level of professionalism.

Of course, this doesn't mean you have to wear a suit to the grocery store, but it also doesn't mean cut-off shorts and a wife beater either. It is important to have self-confidence and pride about who you are, what you represent, and how you want others to perceive you. Part of that is about how you present yourself while you are out in public. Imagine the President of the United States out in the public eye. How does he present himself? Hold yourself to a similar standard; you are worth it. After all, he probably has a "wife beater" that he wears at home, too, he keeps it at home. So should you.

Mental Health

I never truly understood the importance of mental health until I had children. Any parent who takes raising their child seriously understands how incredibly taxing this feat really is. Of course, it's worth it, and that is why we work so hard at it. That being said, it can be a constant drain on your mental health. While everybody's situation is unique, here are a few things I do to maintain my mental health, and a few key principles I think are sound as well.

Obviously for myself, my martial arts training is a big part of my mental health, energy, and focus. Although some of my classes are spent teaching kids, they are not my kids so it is a lot easier to get them to listen to me. In fact, I tell parents of my students to use me as an example as needed at their own home. "What would Sensei think about you doing that?" is one that I hear of a lot. Benefits I get from teaching are working on continual improvement, helping others grow, and I cannot emphasize enough what an outlet it is to punch and kick on a bag on a regular basis. Whether it is in the martial arts or not, I highly encourage some sort of routine and regular workout program.

Other things that I enjoy for my sanity include writing, reading, shooting, archery, and going for a ride on my motorcycle. They are things I can enjoy by myself or with friends, and they interest and entertain me. This is the critical point – they interest and entertain me. I am the type of person who feels guilty when I am entertained. I feel as if I should be working on something more productive. However, I find that when I take some time out for myself, my productivity levels are much higher. One might argue that he or she can't take time to sleep because it takes away from productivity time, but go a couple of days without sleep and see how productive you are. As with many things, find the balance.

Balance, again, is key here. We are all unique, so there is no right answer. However, there is one set of principles that seemed to work well in my household. Finding your balance within this concept I'm sure will prove beneficial to you. In my family, we call it the "You time, Me time, Us time, Family time." One weekend day a month, I have to find something to do on my own, guilt-free. The same goes for my wife. This way we can plan to have that time, and most importantly, as I said, it's guilt-free. We function very well as a family unit. We enjoy being together, doing things together, and even doing nothing together. We know, though, that we have to find the proper balance in our family unit now, so that it doesn't balance itself out against our will later, which would be almost certainly inevitable. We also take time to go out as a couple once every six to eight weeks. There are scheduled events that come up in between those times, dinner events, fundraisers, meetings, etc., but our couple night is set up for purely our enjoyment. Oftentimes it is dinner and a movie. This allows us to not wake up as strangers in eighteen years. You may laugh, but I've seen it happen. The family unit is very demanding, and it is important to be fully in it when you are in it, and to be sure to take some breaks from it.

Family time is always our default time spender. As I mentioned, we enjoy this role. It is truly a forced effort to create balance on the "You, Me, and Us times." We work it out, though, and even make a conscious effort to take it a step further. We feel that it is important to us as parents to have some "one on one" time with our children. We've found great pleasure in creating a "date" day once a week. One morning a week, my wife will take our son out to do something special, and I will stay home and do something special with our daughter. The next week I'll take our son out while my wife stays home with our daughter. The following week I will take our daughter out to do something special, and the week after that I will stay home and do something special with our son.

This balance has been great for all of us. We all enjoy our time out with each other doing different things. It also gives our kids (and us) great exposure to different "gender-typed" activities. Our kids are young enough that they don't much care about gender-specific activities, but we know that time will come. Since we are budget conscious, we often go to our local zoo or discovery center. We have annual memberships at both of these places, so we can frequent them as often as we like without adding to our expenses. As the kids get older, this will be a great teaching opportunity as well about budgets, expenses, and entertainment. Our memberships include both indoor and outdoor activities, so we're covered for all seasons.

Financial Security

Let me start this section by encouraging everyone to take a hard look at their financial status, goals, and ambitions. It is truly sad that our country and many of us as individuals are a poor financial situation. Please take a look at your situation and make adjustments as needed, if needed. Many people believe the pursuit of money is evil. I couldn't disagree more. In fact, I would liken that statement as being the same as saying that the pursuit of food is evil. This is, of course, absurd since we need food in order to survive. The hunter / gatherer society hunted and gathered as a means to their survival. In today's socioeconomic society, we typically must acquire money in order to survive. The pursuit of it, and educating ourselves about it, is our need and responsibility.

Many of us, if we are lucky, live a "paycheck to paycheck" type of lifestyle. I say "if we are lucky" because many people have acquired large amounts of high interest bad debt, with little or no means of getting out of their indebted situations. Financial security and asset/wealth accumulation is hard, even when you're focusing on it. Don't focus on it, and it is almost impossible. I am speaking from my humble point of view. There are many out there who will claim they know a lot more than I do on the subject, and still many that actually do. That being said, I will give you a simple little secret to being wealthy. I call it Wealth 101, or the "hamburger / steak" scenario. Here is how it goes.

Can afford the hamburger but orders the steak = poor / indebted

Can afford the steak and orders the steak = paycheck to paycheck

Can afford the steak but orders the hamburger = wealthy

(download your copy of this Wealth 101 equation at www.womantalkbook.com under the "forms and pics" tab)

This is, of course, an oversimplified scenario, but it is important to understand that this "mindset" is what allows for wealth through interest, investments, savings, and asset accumulation. You will allow yourself to take potential excess and turn it into wealth. The math side of it is easy. The societal and psychological side of it is challenging.

The reason I say the latter of these two scenarios is challenging is because it requires the necessary discipline to make it happen. We often hold ourselves less accountable to ourselves than we do to other people. We cut ourselves some "slack." The world is hard enough sometimes. I "deserve" to have a steak, whether I can't afford it, think I can afford it, or can afford it. The discipline to overcome our daily obstacles and battles pertaining to finance has to be driven by a much larger force. That is why its focus needs to be part of your mission statement or "slices of pie."

When my wife and I got married, we had a net worth of essentially zero. Both of us were in school, studying hard, and finding ways to pay for our education. We knew this situation was temporary, and we discussed how important it was for us to develop some financial security, so we would have options. We decided that if there was any material purchase that meant more to us than our financial security, we should go ahead and buy in now so we didn't have to dwell on it. We sat down with pen and paper and couldn't come up with anything. Since then we have been on a "hamburger ordering" path to accumulating wealth and financial security. It is one of our slices of Pie, and DEMANDS our attention every year, every month, every week, every day. Are we suffering, deprived? Far from it. In fact, we live quite comfortably, and our lifestyle improves as our wealth, net worth, and cash flow does. That said, it improves relative to our financial goals.

Since I sold my company at the end of 2011, I have been able to stay at home with my kids before they start school. My wife works three days a week, and enjoys four days in a row every week with me and the kids. We visit her hometown of Prague every year three weeks at a time. We purchased an apartment for cash in Prague. We are truly enjoying some downtime with our children before they start school, and we are doing this while continuing to increase our net worth and meeting our financial goals. Once the kids are in school, we can get back to being even more aggressive with our goals, while still maintaining our current lifestyle.

The real trick is to understand one basic underlying human instinct. We often have a natural instinct to work our way to zero. Take an individual who makes $20,000 a year. That individual is more than likely broke. Now take an individual who makes $100,000 a year. That individual is more than likely broke too. The second individual might have more "toys," but is still broke from a net worth point of view. If you give the first individual the second individual's income, you would think they would be set! However, more than likely, that's not the case. In fact, they may be worse off trying to manage that kind of money than if you left them with the 20,000, since they haven't worked through the process of how to acquire it.

The real trick is to understand that you are in control. When my wife and I started making more money as we got older, my mother knew we were very committed to our financial goals. She encouraged us to take some time to ourselves and splurge on "us" a little bit. I told her I thought this was a valid point, and that I agreed with her philosophy. I shared with her some of the things we did to *splurge on us*. Her comment was that "you have so much more money than before, you should do something more." There lies the trouble. That is the trap we often fall into, and why we always find ourselves hovering around "zero."

I quickly informed my mother of an individual I knew who made sure he took time for himself. Although he made very little money, only about $10,000 a year, he made it a point to go to the movies once a month. He would find what he wants to watch, go to the movies, order popcorn and a drink, and truly enjoy himself. My mother, slightly confused that I was making her point for her, stated "See, that's what I'm talking about. You have to do things for yourself." I then let her know of another individual I know. He made around a million dollars a year, but he made it a point to go to the movies once a month. He would find what he wants to watch, go to the movies, order popcorn and a drink, and truly enjoy himself. My mother's comment was that he could do so much more. My point, however, was that it was possible to derive equal amounts of enjoyment and satisfaction out of this same activity. It is the relativity that makes situations ambiguous and complicated. If you have a bigger drive and goal in mind, then it helps keep ambiguity and complication in check.

The key thing here is to have a plan, have goals, and have a TEAMMATE while trying to accomplish them. If you and your spouse are not on board with the same objective, then failure is simply a matter of time. As I mentioned earlier, my wife, Lida, and I sat down and made our plan. We both committed to it, and we both own it. Therefore, we both make decisions in our lives that keep us aligned with it. For many people, many purchasing decisions come from external factors in their lives. Robert Kiyosaki, author of *Rich Dad Poor Dad* defined it best. He states that "We spend money we don't have, to buy things we don't need, to impress people we don't like." That is a perfect saying. Without a plan and financial goals, it is my belief that in an attempt to get to "zero," you will fall face first into this saying.

I have a friend and business partner who really struggled with this early on in our business dealings. I remember visiting him for a meeting with all the partners of our company. We had the meeting in his newly built home. He was very proud of it and gave me the tour. I was happy for him. However, as the tour continued, I got the impression he was trying to impress me with his new home. We sat down in his kitchen, and I proceeded to give him the "I don't give a *verb*" speech. Now, verb was replaced with another word in my speech, I'll let you use your imagination. You can insert your own verb, use an adjective, or even a noun for yourself. The point that I was trying to make to him, though, was that I don't care.

At first, his reaction was much like yours might initially be. What an insensitive jerk, right? Nothing could be further from the truth. I simply stated that he should be very pleased with his accomplishment, but that his accomplishment should be aligned with his own financial and budgetary goals. Mine are inconsequential in comparison. He should "selfishly" do what is best for him and his situation, not be comparing it with anyone else. He had nice new furniture he was very proud of, and it was comfortable too. I informed him, however, if he only had milk crates to sit on I would still sit down and enjoy his company and our meeting. I told him that anyone who thought differently, he should eliminate from his life. It is very easy to get into the "keep up with the Jones' mentality." Having a plan and goals, coupled with the "I don't give a *verb*" attitude, should hopefully keep you in check and on track.

Tools for Success in Finance

As I have already stated, you absolutely must have some financial plans and goals. I am not talking about a general idea rattling around somewhere up in your head. I'm talking about pen to paper, as specific as possible plans and goals. It is important to have a one-year, five-year, and ten-year plan. Without it, you will just go day to day. What you focus on grows. Focus on where you would like to be financially, and then start a well-thought-out, intelligent plan on how to get there. *(Go to www.womantalkbook.com and click on the "forms and pics" tab to get printable sheets for marking down your goals)*

Once you have your plans in place, consult the professionals. I say this for two reasons from two perspectives. The first reason is that it is important to consult with professionals in the field such as accountants, attorneys, and brokers for implementation of your financial goals. "Murphy" is always lingering around, waiting for the person who is ill-prepared. Don't give Murphy the opportunity to land on you. Communicate with these professionals what your goals are, and make a strategic plan of attack on how you are going to accomplish them. This is, again, why it is important to be as specific as possible. The more information they have, the better they can serve you. This often comes at a price, but it is marginal, and should be considered money well spent to help you achieve your goals.

The second reason is so that you can make educated and informed decisions without the influence of outsiders. For example, let's say you sit down and look at your budget, and you decide that you are going to purchase a home. Most people I talk to go and ask the bank how much money they will loan them, and then purchase a home at that price (or often 10% higher than that). Not that there is necessarily anything wrong with this, but I would encourage you to look at the perspective differences between you and the bank. The bank is going to look at your income, and from that determine what is the maximum amount they can lend you so you can pay it back as slowly as possible with as high as interest as possible. This makes the "ugly" sheet (on your end) look pretty to them. The bank is only looking at "nonspecific" information. The bank doesn't know your financial goals. Upon looking at your own financial goals, you may decide that half of all the money you bring in is going to go toward investing, before it ever reaches your "pocket." So based off of that knowledge, you know that the most you can spend on a mortgage is $1500 a month. The bank, however, looks at your "financials" and tells you that you can afford $3000 a month. This may be true, but it is not congruent with your financial plan. So be smarter than that, and don't give in to being overspent. Make your own calculations, and then go from there.

Start the habit of saving. I remember reading that somewhere when I was very young. The statement was "Even if it is only $10 a month, start saving." This seemed like a silly statement to me, because that only accumulated $120 within a year's time (without any growth). As I got older and more experienced, I understood the meaning behind this simple statement. It is truly geared toward development of the habit. It's easy for us to put off saving. The concept of saving becomes a perpetual *when*. *When* I get that raise I will save, *when* I pay off this bill I will save, *when, when, when.*

I've got news for you, *when* never comes. You'll already be working hard toward attaining your "zero" when *when* comes along. Therefore, it is truly the habit of saving that really counts. Like many things, the first step is the hardest. It might sound silly, but start with $10. You may quickly realize you can easily contribute more, so do it. You will already have the process started. You'll have an amount to increase, you'll have a place to put it, and you'll have developed the habit. I am a big fan of automatic payments. I dollar cost average many stocks, and I do this by automatically having an amount come out of our pay that goes straight to my financial advisor. Then, as I work toward my "zero," that amount is already out there working for me.

These are some very basic, humble suggestions. To many of you, this may be common knowledge. To others, this may be greatly beneficial. Like everything else in this book, take what you can use and discard the rest. However, I truly believe that if you put these tools and concepts to work, you can only improve your financial situation. Like many things in life, there is no right answer. You have to develop and work on the process as you go, incorporating all of the variables that make you uniquely you. However, it all starts with the implementation of habits and the growth of your knowledge, so get to it if you haven't already.

As I mentioned earlier, all of this should be a committed team effort with your spouse. If a couple commits to this, focuses on it, and moves forward with it, it is hard for me to imagine not being successful with it. Can you imagine how a divorce would impact this strong movement forward? The team would be broken. Combined assets would have to be separated. The synergy behind these assets and the couple would be destroyed. I cannot imagine having to separate that *team* once it is in place. Perhaps that is one reason why the divorce rate is lower for these individuals. This is one more component, I truly believe, this helps a couple stay together. This is a very pleasant *side effect* that you can benefit from in having this put in place.

I have in my net worth calculation spreadsheet the phrase "Reflect on the Past, Plan for the Future, Live in the Moment." This is a philosophy that came to me years ago, and one I try to live every day. The past is gone, no need to dwell on it, but I can learn from it. The future has yet to come, but I had better be preparing for it. However, nothing in the future is guaranteed, so I had better be living in the moment. This, for me, is the proper balance of how I should live my life for myself and my family, and I do so to the best of my ability. I encourage you to do the same, if you're not already.

*(For more strategies on personal finance and increasing your net worth, you can order my co-authored book **"Change One Thing: Take Your First Steps Towards Massive Success"** from the www.womantalk.com website. You can also text the word "wealth" to 785-222-4007 to download a **free copy** of my **Financial Workbook**)*

Spiritual Fulfillment

This brings us to our last "slice of pie," spiritual fulfillment. In much the way that there is no right answer for financial security, there is even less of a right answer for spiritual fulfillment. At least *math* is involved in financial security. Man (sorry women, you know I mean "people" kind) has long been in search of the self. From philosophy, to religion, to science, we are constantly in search of the "great beyond." Very few of us are comfortable with the concept that we are born to die. Therefore, we create these vehicles that help define our existence.

Your own beliefs are probably something you hold dear. Some are proud to share their beliefs with others. Still some are prone to keep their beliefs to themselves. One key thing that we should all remember is there is no right answer. I say this to encourage everyone to be open to other people's beliefs and points of view. Beliefs are exactly as they are defined, they are beliefs. They are the comprised opinion that one forms from their prolonged exposure and experience(s) to given situations.

I took a class in college called World Religions. In the class the professor indicated that there are over 1,800 different religions in the United States alone. He further commented that to think you have the right one was a statement of utmost arrogance. I don't say this to ruffle feathers or to downplay anyone's beliefs, I simply say it to encourage everyone to keep an open mind.

We could sit down right now, try to define our own religion, and come up with the most absurd belief structure that we could think of. Unfortunately, we would probably not be unique because that "religion" we would design is probably already out there somewhere. It probably also has many followers.

It is extremely difficult for many people to discuss their personal beliefs with other people, especially if those other people's beliefs don't coincide with theirs. If this is your situation and you cannot fathom or appreciate other people's beliefs, then I strongly encourage you to keep your beliefs to yourself. This will save you a lot of energy trying to reason and rationalize a belief. If you can keep an open mind and be objective, then by all means "share away."

It took me a long time to understand why belief structures could be the gateway drug to such heated arguments and conflicting dispositions. I only understood when I learned emotions are twenty-four times more powerful than logic. When you look at something that isn't able to be "proved," it can only be managed by your belief system. If we sit down and "rationalize" a hypothesis that can be proved, then it can be a relatively calm discussion of back and forth understanding. Enter into the equation something that is not verifiable, and then we are amped up twenty-four times on differing beliefs that have no solvable outcomes. Heated argument and conflicting disposition is the only logical outcome.

My point is simply this. We are all human, and all that implies. None of us are right insofar as having a claimed knowledge or proof on our divinity. We are only a sum total of our beliefs. The most important thing to understand is that some things work for some people, other things work for others. It is critical to have an inherent respect for what works for us, and what works for others. It is hard for us sometimes, but we don't have to be "right." We only need to do and believe what works for us. This, in my humble opinion, is our greatest struggle in the attainment for spiritual fulfillment. We want to search for and obtain the right answers. If someone's answer is different than ours, then our logical nature dismisses it as false or wrong. Two plus two cannot be four and seven. Our left brain understands this. But what if two plus two can be four and seven? Our right brain could ponder this one until the end of time if not interrupted by the left brain. Beliefs are primarily a right-brained activity. Leave them over there and understand their nature, and it should all be good. Don't try to rationalize your "beliefs," it sounds foolish. Just know that they are your beliefs and hold true to them unapologetically.

If you want to have some fun with this concept of "belief," then play around with the concept of love. Love is one of the most powerful, real, and intense emotions that exists. There is no denying its existence, and if you feel it then you know it to be real. That being said, try to rationally prove your love of someone. What you will quickly find out is this cannot be done if it is under the scrutiny of "proof." You cannot "prove" you love someone. Your initial impulse may be to describe what you do for someone, but a rational onlooker will quickly rip your intentions apart. They will say that your actions could be for manipulation, or to be put in the will, or some other means of self-service. As appalling as these accusations may be, you cannot deny their potential validity. Someone could perform the same acts for the reasons indicated instead of for love. And so the challenge to prove love goes on. However, regardless of this continued attempt to define or prove your love, you know the love you have for those important in your life. Just because you cannot prove it, doesn't make it any less real. Know what you know, and believe what you believe, without being burdened by attempting to prove it.

To reiterate, the key thing here in your own spiritual fulfillment is to do what works for you. If you find something that does not conflict with your Core Values, does not hurt anyone else, and most importantly makes you happy, then I "believe" you are on the right track. If you believe it to, then who cares what anyone else thinks?

Summing Up

Remember, our goal in life should to be happy and make others happy around us. If you haven't already, read the books that I recommended at the beginning of this chapter. They were *The 7 Habits of Highly Effective People* by Dr. Stephen R. Covey, and *Laws of Success* by Napoleon Hill. It also wouldn't hurt my feelings if you read *Change One Thing: Take Your First Steps Towards Massive Success*. The concepts in these books when implemented will most certainly improve many different aspects of your day to day living.

It would be to your advantage to also sit down and define your Core Values. What is truly important to you? Are you comfortable living paycheck to paycheck, or do you prefer having some sort of investing or saving plan? Are you okay with a spouse who thinks cheating in a relationship is okay, or do you want a monogamous partner? Is trustworthiness important to you? What principles are important to you in your life, and what do you expect from others? You should already have a good idea about this, but I challenge you to revisit the concept and see if there is even room for improvement.

Thank you again for reading. I wish you the best of luck in defining and reaching your dreams and goals. I hope that you can benefit from the information in this bonus chapter. May you find the happiness that you desire, and may you have the ability to laugh off the mistakes that you make along the way towards attaining it.

www.womantalkbook.com

About the Author

Kevin was born and lives in Kansas. He is a loving husband to his wife Lida, and loving father to his two children Kalvin and Klara.

Kevin earned his Business Administration Degree from the University of Washburn. He is a business owner and Instructor in the Martial Arts. He has also co-authored the book "Change One Thing: Take Your First Steps Towards Massive Success."

Kevin is a 5th degree black belt in the Dillman Karate Method. He has received multiple competition awards both locally and nationally. He was also honored with the "Instructor of the Year" award from the United States Martial Arts Hall of Fame in 2006, and "Shorinryu Master of the Year" in 2014. He is currently co-authoring a book on the martial arts "Martial Arts for the Modern World." Kevin is committed to the improvement of individual excellence.

www.ingramcontent.com/pod-product-compliance
Lightning Source LLC
LaVergne TN
LVHW011423080426
835512LV00005B/227